Keynote

2

David Bohlke

NATIONAL GEOGRAPHIC LEARNING | CENGAGE Learning·

Australia • Brazil • Mexico • Singapore • United Kingdom • United States

NATIONAL GEOGRAPHIC LEARNING | CENGAGE Learning

Keynote 2
David Bohlke

Publisher: Andrew Robinson

Executive Editor: Sean Bermingham

Senior Development Editor: Derek Mackrell

Development Editor: Christopher Street

Director of Global Marketing: Ian Martin

Senior Product Marketing Manager:
Caitlin Thomas

IP Analyst: Kyle Cooper

IP Project Manager: Carissa Poweleit

Media Researcher: Leila Hishmeh

Senior Director of Production: Michael Burggren

Senior Content Project Manager: Tan Jin Hock

Manufacturing Planner: Mary Beth Hennebury

Compositor: SPi Global

Cover/Text Design: Brenda Carmichael

Cover Photo: The Park Royal Hotel green terrace
in Singapore: © Patrick Bingham Hall

For product information and technology assistance, contact us at
Cengage Learning Customer & Sales Support, 1-800-354-9706

For permission to use material from this text or product,
submit all requests online at **cengage.com/permissions**
Further permissions questions can be emailed to
permissionrequest@cengage.com

Student Book with My Keynote Online:
ISBN-13: 978-1-337-10411-1

Student Book:
ISBN-13: 978-1-305-96504-1

National Geographic Learning
20 Channel Center Street
Boston, MA 02210
USA

Cengage Learning is a leading provider of customized learning solutions with office locations around the globe, including Singapore, the United Kingdom, Australia, Mexico, Brazil, and Japan. Locate your local office at **international.cengage.com/region**

Cengage Learning products are represented in Canada by Nelson Education, Ltd.

Visit National Geographic Learning online at **NGL.cengage.com**
Visit our corporate website at **www.cengage.com**

Printed in the United States of America
Print Number: 03 Print Year: 2017

Contents

Featured **TED**TALKS

Munir Virani
1 Why I love vultures

A. J. Jacobs
2 The world's largest family reunion

Ann Morgan
3 My year reading a book from every country

Daria van den Bercken
4 Why I take the piano on the road … and in the air

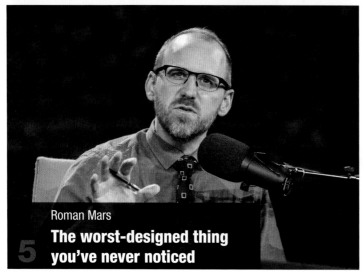

Roman Mars
5 The worst-designed thing you've never noticed

Jarrett J. Krosoczka
6 How a boy became an artist

Andras Forgacs
**Leather and meat
without killing animals**

7

Alessandra Orofino
It's our city. Let's fix it.

8

Joy Sun
**Should you donate
differently?**

9

Tan Le
**A headset that reads your
brainwaves**

10

Louie Schwartzberg
**The hidden beauty of
pollination**

11

Nizar Ibrahim
**How we unearthed the
*Spinosaurus***

12

Scope and Sequence

		LESSON A		LESSON B	
UNIT		**VOCABULARY**	**LISTENING**	**LANGUAGE FOCUS**	**SPEAKING**
1 Protectors		Types of animals	**Moving people to action** *Joel Sartore, photographer*	**Function** Describing events in the present **Grammar** Simple present and present continuous	Protecting species
2 Family Connections		Extended family	**My family history** *Ken Lejtenyi, sales director*	**Function** Talking about future plans **Grammar** Future forms	My family
3 Global Stories		Genres of fiction	**Interview with an author** *Madeleine Thien, author*	**Function** Adding details **Grammar** Relative clauses	Can you guess?

PRESENTATION 1 Talking about an endangered species

4 Music		Music	**A traditional singer** *Iarla Ó Lionáird, singer*	**Function** Talking about quantity **Grammar** Countable and uncountable nouns	Musical preferences
5 Good Design		Design elements	**A designer's advice** *Sarah Lafferty, designer*	**Function** Talking about place and position **Grammar** Prepositions of place	Designing a coat of arms
6 Inspiration		Sources of inspiration	**My inspiration** *Franklin Chang Diaz, former astronaut*	**Function** Reporting what someone said **Grammar** Reported speech	Getting advice

PRESENTATION 2 Describing a favorite teacher

LESSON C	LESSON D		LESSON E	
READING	**TED TALK**	**PRESENTATION SKILLS**	**COMMUNICATE**	**WRITING**
Vultures in danger	**WHY I LOVE VULTURES** *Munir Virani*	Signposting with questions	A group decision	Writing about an endangered species
Genealogy	**THE WORLD'S LARGEST FAMILY REUNION** *A. J. Jacobs*	Personalizing a presentation	Family tree	Writing an invitation
Top picks	**MY YEAR READING A BOOK FROM EVERY COUNTRY** *Ann Morgan*	Closing a presentation	A book recommendation	Writing a book review
Music and the brain	**WHY I TAKE THE PIANO ON THE ROAD ... AND IN THE AIR** *Daria van den Bercken*	Providing background information	Desert island discs	Writing about a favorite song
Symbol of a city	**THE WORST-DESIGNED THING YOU'VE NEVER NOTICED** *Roman Mars*	Numbering key points	A new city flag	Writing about your country's flag
Inspiring lives	**HOW A BOY BECAME AN ARTIST** *Jarrett Krosoczka*	Using your voice effectively	A lively dinner party	Writing about an inspiring person

Scope and Sequence

UNIT	LESSON A		LESSON B	
	VOCABULARY	**LISTENING**	**LANGUAGE FOCUS**	**SPEAKING**
7 Ethical Choices	Ethical food choices	**Sustainable chef** *Barton Seaver, chef*	**Function** Making predictions **Grammar** *Will* for predictions	Predicting future habits
8 Better Cities	Features of a city	**Living abroad** *Claire Street, expatriate*	**Function** Using phrasal verbs **Grammar** Phrasal verbs	Talking about best places
9 Giving	Helping others	**My fundraising adventure** *Neil Glover, fundraiser*	**Function** Making offers and describing real conditions **Grammar** *Will* for offers and conditions	Planning an event

PRESENTATION 3 Describing a great city

UNIT	LESSON A		LESSON B	
10 Mind and Machine	Brain functions	**The power of visualization** *Brian Scholl, professor*	**Function** Using adverbial phrases **Grammar** Adverbial phrases	A logic puzzle
11 Nature	Nature	**My experiences in nature** *Tony Gainsford, nature lover*	**Function** Talking about past experiences **Grammar** Present perfect	Experiences in nature
12 Discovery	Discoveries	**An amazing find** *Fredrik Hiebert, archeologist*	**Function** Talking about discoveries **Grammar** Passive	Discovery quiz

PRESENTATION 4 Talking about an amazing discovery

LESSON C	LESSON D		LESSON E		
READING	**TED TALK**	**PRESENTATION SKILLS**	**COMMUNICATE**	**WRITING**	
Leather from a lab	**LEATHER AND MEAT WITHOUT KILLING ANIMALS** *Andras Forgacs*	Creating effective slides	Weighing both sides	Writing about the future of food	
Connecting citizens	**IT'S OUR CITY. LET'S FIX IT.** *Alessandra Orofino*	Using anecdotes	Let's fix this!	Writing about a change for the better	
Donation revolution	**SHOULD YOU DONATE DIFFERENTLY?** *Joy Sun*	Using supporting evidence	How to give	Writing about a charity you support	
Power of the mind	**A HEADSET THAT READS YOUR BRAINWAVES** *Tan Le*	Dealing with the unexpected	A new product	Writing a proposal	
The miracle of pollen	**THE HIDDEN BEAUTY OF POLLINATION** *Louie Schwartzberg*	Calling others to action	Nature weekend	Writing a blog post	
The dinosaur hunter	**HOW WE UNEARTHED THE *SPINOSAURUS*** *Nizar Ibrahim*	Using descriptive language	A newspaper interview	Writing a news report	

Welcome to Keynote!

In this book, you will develop your English language skills and explore great ideas with an authentic TED Talk. Each unit topic is based around a TED speaker's main idea.

In Unit 8, Alessandra Orofino introduces her organization, which connects citizens and helps them initiate change in their city.

LISTENING AND SPEAKING

- Practice listening to real people talking about the unit topic. Real-life people featured in this book include a singer, a designer, and an archeologist.

- Develop your **speaking confidence** with a model conversation and guided speaking tasks.

  See pages 89, 91

VOCABULARY AND GRAMMAR

- In each unit, you'll learn key words, phrases, and grammar structures for talking about the unit topic.

- Build **language and visual literacy skills** with real-life information—in Unit 8, you'll learn about four of the happiest cities in the world.

  See page 90

READING

- Develop your **reading and vocabulary skills** with a specially adapted reading passage. In Unit 8, you'll learn how technology is helping improve lives in Rio de Janeiro.

- The passage includes several words and phrases that appear later in the TED Talk.

  See pages 92–93

VIEWING

- Practice your viewing and **critical thinking** skills as you watch a specially adapted TED Talk.

- Notice how TED speakers use effective language and **communication** skills to present their ideas.

  See pages 94–95

COMMUNICATING AND PRESENTING

- Use your **creativity** and **collaboration skills** in a final task that reviews language and ideas from the unit.

  See page 96

- Build your **speaking confidence** further in a Presentation task (after every three units).

  See page 107

WRITING

- Communicate your own ideas about the unit topic in a controlled writing task.

  See page 96

- Develop your **writing and language skills** further in the **Keynote Workbook** and online at **MyKeynoteOnline**.

What is **TED**?

TED has a simple goal: to spread great ideas. Every year, hundreds of presenters share ideas at TED events around the world. Millions of people watch TED Talks online. The talks inspire many people to change their attitudes and their lives.

SPREADING IDEAS WORLDWIDE

Over **10,000**
TEDx events in
167 countries

Over **2,200**
TEDTALKS recorded

TEDTALKS
translated into
105 languages

Over
1,000,000,000
views of **TED**TALKS at TED.com

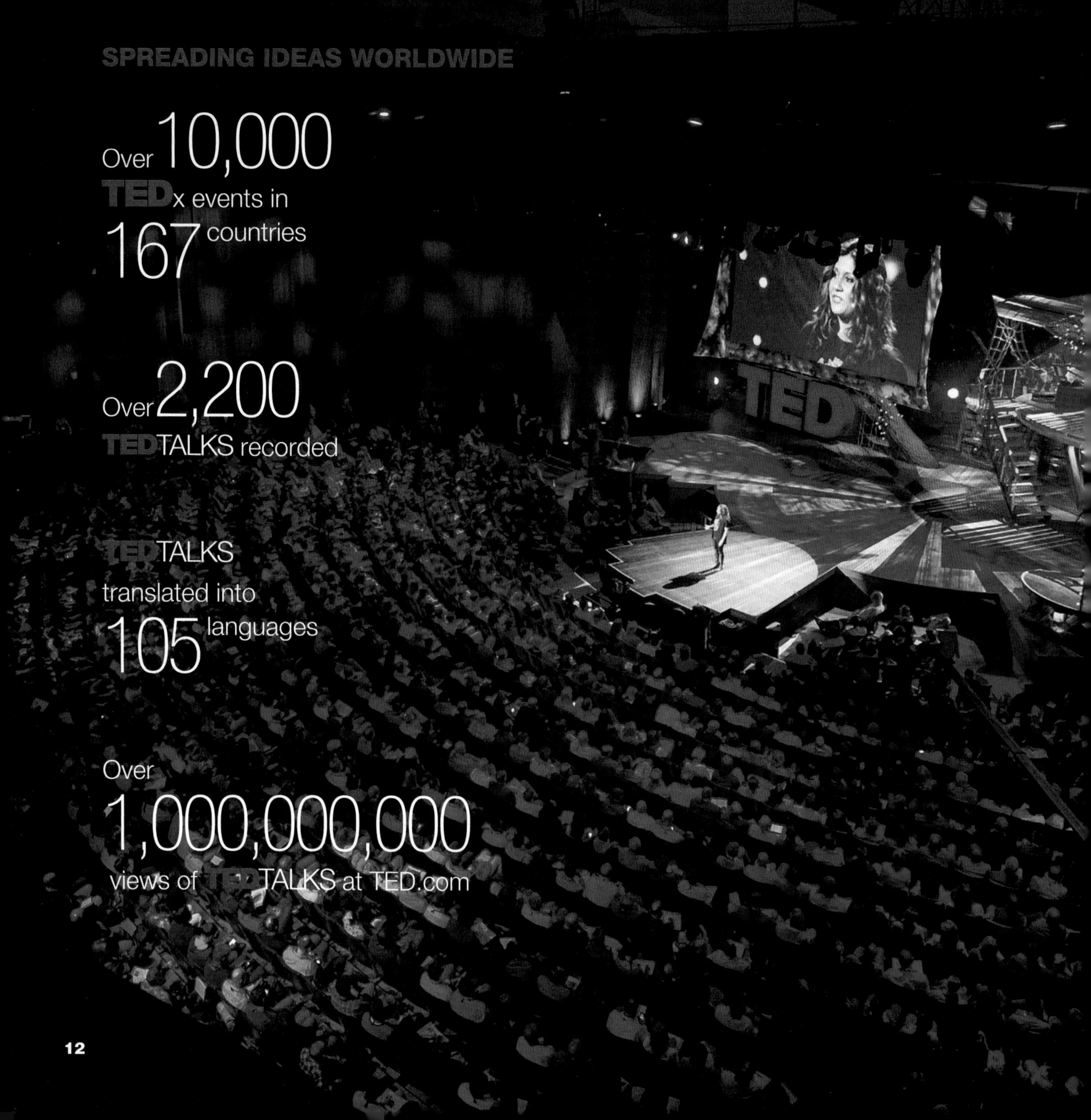

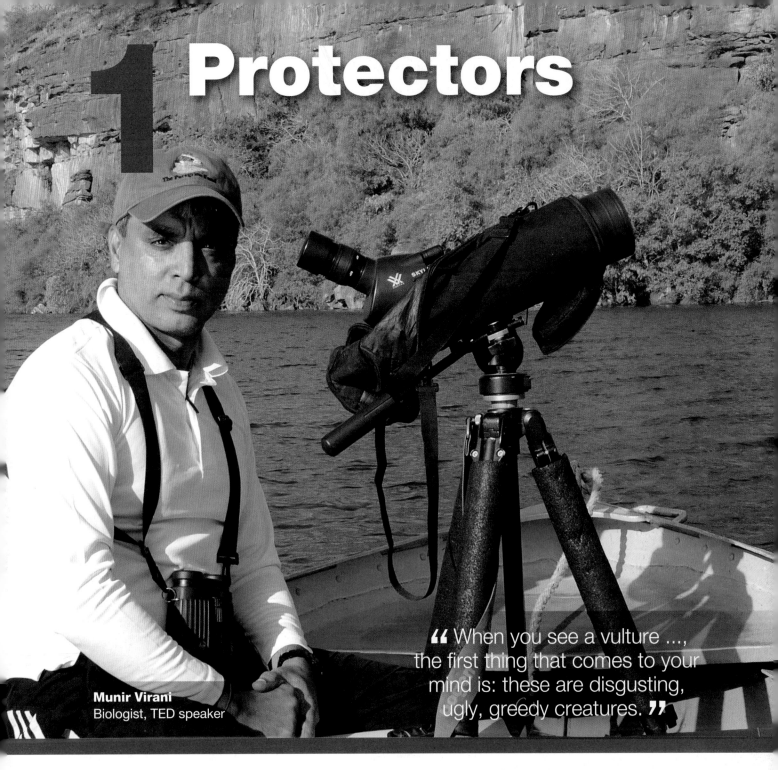

1 Protectors

Munir Virani
Biologist, TED speaker

" When you see a vulture ...,
the first thing that comes to your
mind is: these are disgusting,
ugly, greedy creatures. "

UNIT GOALS

In this unit, you will ...

- talk about endangered and threatened animals.
- read about why vulture numbers are declining.
- watch a TED Talk about the importance of saving vultures.

WARM UP

▶ **1.1** Watch part of Munir Virani's TED Talk. Answer the questions with a partner.

1 Why do you think vultures are threatened?

2 What's your impression of vultures? Do you agree with Virani?

A critically endangered Indochinese box turtle photographed by Joel Sartore as part of his Photo Ark project

1A Animals under threat

VOCABULARY Types of animals

A Read the paragraph about Joel Sartore's Photo Ark project. Complete the table with the words in **bold**.

Joel Sartore's Photo Ark project started with endangered **amphibians**. Sartore wanted to do something to show these species to the world before they were gone forever. Soon, Sartore heard about other species in trouble—**mammals, reptiles, birds, fish, insects**. Now, he photographs anything that will stay still long enough for him to take a photo.

Amphibians					
frogs toads	turtles crocodiles	butterflies ants	owls flamingos	sharks tuna	tigers pandas

B Work with a partner. Add one more animal to each of the categories in the table.

C What animals do you know that are endangered? Discuss with a partner.

I think most species of tigers are endangered.

Yeah, I think you're right.

LISTENING Moving people to action

A **1.2** Watch photographer Joel Sartore talking about the Photo Ark. What does he mean when he talks about "moving people to action?"

Photographer Joel Sartore

B ▶ **1.2** Watch again. Complete the sentences with the words you hear.

1 "My goal is to get people to wake up and say 'Whoa! That's _____ !'"

2 "I shoot _____ pictures a year, minimum."

3 "Maybe _____ are keepers."

C CRITICAL THINKING

Evaluating Do you agree that photographs can "move people to action?" Discuss with a partner.

SPEAKING Talking about endangered animals

A ▶ **1.3** What is the biggest threat to the Sumatran elephant?

A: Hey! Check out these elephants.

B: Cool! Are they African elephants?

A: No, they're Sumatran elephants. Oh, how awful. It says here that they are facing extinction.   are endangered / could become extinct

B: That's terrible. Does it say why?

A: Um … it's mostly because people are cutting down the rain forest. But another reason is that people illegally hunt   illegal hunting / poaching
and kill them.

B: How many are there in the wild?   remain / still live

A: Let's see … between 2,400 and 2,800.

B: They're such beautiful animals. I really hope people can find a way to save them.   help / protect

B Practice the conversation with a partner. Practice again using the words on the right.

C Work with a partner to make notes about an endangered animal. Join another pair and share your information.

Animal	Where do they live?	Why are they endangered?

Mountain gorillas live in Africa.

Yeah, and they're endangered because they're losing their habitat.

15

1B How we're helping

LANGUAGE FOCUS Discussing conservation status

A ▷ **1.4** Read the information. Why do you think reindeer populations are healthy?

RISKS OF EXTINCTION

Many animals are facing threats to their survival. The International Union for Conservation of Nature uses a scale to track the conservation status of our world's animal species.

Least concern	Near threatened	Vulnerable	Endangered	Critically endangered	Extinct

Reindeer have a healthy population of around 3.8 million.

Polar bears are vulnerable due to climate change. Only around 20,000 remain.

Sumatran orangutans are in great danger of extinction due to habitat loss. Only 7,500 remain.

West African black rhinos were declared extinct in 2011. The main cause was poaching.

B ▷ **1.5** Listen to an expert talk about three species of fish. Write the conservation status of each one.

1 barracuda: _____

2 bigeye tuna: _____

3 silver trout: _____

C ▷ **1.6** Watch and study the language in the chart.

Describing events in the present	
Every year, the Arctic freezes and melts. Polar bears live in the Arctic. Polar bears hunt seals. Does a vulnerable species have any living individuals? Does an extinct species have any living individuals?	Yes, it does. No, it doesn't.
Our planet's temperature is rising. Polar bears are now losing their hunting grounds. These days, polar bear numbers are declining. Is the world's climate changing? Is the Earth's temperature falling? Why are polar bear numbers decreasing?	Yes, it is. No, it isn't. Because it's harder for them to hunt seals.

For more information on **simple present** and **present continuous**, see Grammar Summary 1 on page 155.

D Match each question to the best response.

1	Do orangutans live in Southeast Asia?	○	○ Yes, it does.
2	Where do they spend most of their time?	○	○ Yes, they do.
3	Are their numbers declining?	○	○ They're trying to protect the forests.
4	Why are the numbers dropping?	○	○ They usually live in trees.
5	What are people doing to protect them?	○	○ It's mainly because of habitat loss.
6	Does poaching threaten them, too?	○	○ Yes, they are.

E Circle the correct words.

1 The green sea turtle (**gets** / **is getting**) its name from the color of its skin.

2 On average, they (**live** / **are living**) up to 80 years.

3 Every year, they (**lay** / **are laying**) thousands of eggs on Florida's beaches.

4 Because of laws protecting their nesting sites, their numbers (**rise** / **are rising**).

5 The U.S. Fish and Wildlife Service (**considers** / **is considering**) changing their status from endangered to threatened.

F ▶ **1.7** Complete the information with the correct form of the words in the box. Listen and check your answers.

do	have	kill	(not) hurt	rise	(not) want

Every year, poachers ¹_____ over 1,000 rhinos in southern Africa. They hunt them for their horns because some people believe the horns ²_____ special medicinal value. The Rhino Rescue Project ³_____ something about it. They are able to make the horn lose its value. But how?

They inject a poison into the horns of living animals. The poison ⁴_____ the rhino, but it makes the horn useless as medicine. Consumers ⁵_____ horns that can make them feel sick. These actions are working. Rhino numbers ⁶_____ slowly.

SPEAKING Protecting species

A Work with a partner. What do you know about these two animal species?

Bengal tigers	kiwis

B You are going to learn about these species. **Student A:** Turn to page 141. **Student B:** Turn to page 142.

Without protection, many believe vultures could soon be extinct.

1C Vultures in danger

PRE-READING Predicting

Discuss with a partner. Why do you think vultures might be in danger? Check your ideas as you read the passage.

▶ 1.8

1   In the early 1990s, something began to happen to India's vultures. Once, tens of millions of these birds filled the skies. Then, suddenly, they began to die out. In less than a decade, the three most common Indian vulture species declined by more than 95 percent. The Oriental white-backed vulture population—once the most common large bird of prey[1] in the world—fell by an incredible 99.9 percent. It was one of the fastest population collapses of any bird species in history.

2   Scientists eventually traced the cause of the decline to a pain-killing drug called diclofenac, which was used to **treat** sick livestock. Although safe for cows, it is deadly to vultures. Any vulture feeding on the flesh[2] of a cow treated with diclofenac soon becomes ill. Millions of vultures died as a result. To stop the decline, India's **government** banned the drug's use on animals in 2006. Today, the country's vulture decline is slowing.

3   Conservationists are now **worried** something similar may be happening in Africa. The continent has already lost one of its eleven vulture species, and seven others are endangered. As with India, a major threat is poisoning. In rural **communities**, it is **common** for herders to lose cows and other livestock to predators. When a lion attacks and kills a cow, the farmers often put poison in the cow's carcass.[3] This kills the lion when it returns to feed. However, vultures also die from the poison when they feed off a poisoned carcass. Researchers believe this may be the cause of over 60 percent of vulture deaths across Africa.

4   Hopefully, Africa can learn from India's recent successes. Vultures may not be cute, say conservationists, but they are one of nature's most important scavengers.[4] Without protection, Africa's vultures may be extinct within the next 50 to 100 years.

---

[1] **bird of prey:** *n.* a bird that eats other animals
[2] **flesh:** *n.* the soft part of the body between the bones and skin

[3] **carcass:** *n.* the body of a dead animal
[4] **scavenger:** *n.* an animal that eats dead animals or plants

UNDERSTANDING GIST

According to the passage, which of these best describes vultures?

a birds that spread diseases

b endangered birds that need our help

c the African lion's best friend

d the strangest of all bird species

UNDERSTANDING MAIN IDEAS

Match the paragraph with the main question it answers. One question is extra.

1 Paragraph 1 ○

2 Paragraph 2 ○

3 Paragraph 3 ○

4 Paragraph 4 ○

○ Why are vulture numbers in Africa declining?

○ Why did vulture populations decline in India?

○ Why is it important to protect Africa's vultures?

○ What will happen to India's vultures in the future?

○ What happened to India's vultures in the 1990s?

UNDERSTANDING CAUSE AND EFFECT

Why have vulture numbers declined? Use the sentences (**a–f**) to complete the summary.

a A farmer places poison inside a cow's dead body.

b People give a drug to sick cows.

c Vultures eventually die due to diclofenac poisoning.

d Both lions and vultures feed on a cow, and they die from poisoning.

e A lion attacks and kills a cow, so the herder decides to kill the lion.

f Vultures start to get sick after they feed on a cow treated with medicine.

India: _____ → _____ → _____   Africa: _____ → _____ → _____

BUILDING VOCABULARY

A Match each word in **blue** from the passage to its definition.

1 treat ○

2 worried ○

3 common ○

4 community ○

5 government ○

○ the group of people who control a country

○ usual; happening often

○ thinking about future problems

○ a group of people who live in the same area

○ to try to make a sick person or animal well again

B CRITICAL THINKING

Reflecting Discuss the questions with a partner.

1 What might be some ways to protect the vultures in Africa?

2 What are some other ways farmers could protect their cows instead of using poison?

1D Why I love vultures

TEDTALKS

Biologist **MUNIR VIRANI** does not want people to think of vultures as **greedy** or ugly **creatures**. Instead, he wants people to understand the **ecological** services they provide. His idea worth spreading is that vultures are **vital** to the environment and to human health, and deserve to be protected.

PREVIEWING

Read the paragraph above. Match each **bold** word to its meaning. You will hear these words in the TED Talk.

1 extremely important: _____

2 animals of any type: _____

3 environmental: _____

4 wanting more than needed: _____

VIEWING

A ▶ **1.9** Watch Part 1 of the TED Talk. Complete the notes.

Generally viewed negatively by society	Two types	Importance of vultures
• Darwin described turkey vultures as "disgusting birds." • Disney has often portrayed vultures as ¹_____ characters.	• New World vultures: mainly found in ²_____ • Old World vultures: ³_____ out of 16 species are at high risk of extinction	• clean up animal carcasses and help control the spread of ⁴_____

B ▶ **1.10** Watch Part 2 of the TED Talk. Circle the correct option to complete each sentence.

1 People are doing research to find out (**where vultures go** / **what vultures eat**).

2 Virani says that saving vultures is a(n) (**local** / **international**) problem.

3 Virani says we can all help by (**visiting zoos to learn** / **educating people**) about vultures.

4 Darwin changed his mind about vultures when he watched them (**fly** / **clean up a carcass**).

C CRITICAL THINKING

Reflecting Has your opinion of vultures changed after watching Virani's TED Talk? Discuss with a partner.

VOCABULARY IN CONTEXT

▶ **1.11** Watch the excerpts from the TED Talk. Choose the correct meaning of the words.

PRESENTATION SKILLS Signposting with questions

> One useful way to organize a presentation is to begin each major part by asking the audience a question. This helps the audience know exactly what you are going to talk about.

A ▶ **1.12** Watch the excerpt. Complete the question Virani asked near the start of his presentation.

"First of all, _____ such a bad press?"

B ▶ **1.13** Match the questions Virani asks with the responses he gives. Watch and check your answers.

1 So why are vultures important? ○	○	You can become active, make noise.
2 So what is the problem with vultures? ○	○	First of all, they provide vital ecological services.
3 So what's being done? ○	○	Well, we're conducting research on these birds.
4 How can you help? ○	○	We have eight species of vultures that occur in Kenya of which six are highly threatened with extinction

C Imagine you are going to give a presentation on pandas. Write three key points about them. Then exchange notes with a partner. Write a signposting question for each key point.

Key points

1 _____ .

2 _____ .

3 _____ .

Questions

_____ ?

_____ ?

_____ ?

A palm-nut vulture in flight,
Bioko Island, Equatorial Guinea

COMMUNICATE A group decision

A Work with a partner. Look at the photos of endangered species below. Guess the names of the animals.

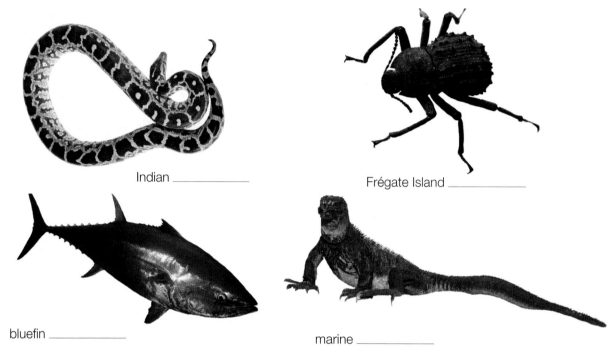

Indian _____

Frégate Island _____

bluefin _____

marine _____

B Work in groups of four. You are members of an organization that raises money to protect endangered species. **Student A:** Turn to page 141. **Student B:** Turn to page 142. **Student C:** Turn to page 144. **Student D:** Turn to page 146. Read the information and make notes about your animal.

C Your organization only has enough money to help save one animal. Use your notes and take turns presenting the information you learned about your animal to your group. Then, work together to choose the one animal you are going to save.

> **Presenting arguments**
> *For one thing ...*   *Something else to consider is ...*   *The most important thing is ...*

D Compare your group's decision with others in the class. Which animal was most popular? Why do you think this was the case?

WRITING An endangered species

Write about an animal you think needs protection.

> An animal that needs our protection is the polar bear. Rising sea levels are threatening its survival. We have a responsibility to save polar bears because humans caused climate change.

2 Family Connections

> **"** All of you have famous people and historical figures in your tree, because we are all connected … **"**

A. J. Jacobs
Writer, TED speaker

UNIT GOALS

In this unit, you will …

- talk about your immediate and extended family.
- read about researching family trees.
- watch a TED Talk about how we are all connected.

WARM UP

▶ **2.1** Watch part of A. J. Jacobs's TED Talk. Answer the questions with a partner.

1 What does Jacobs mean when he says, "we are all connected"?

2 What do you think is the importance of a world family tree?

A family reunites at a Christmas party.

2A Family ties

VOCABULARY Extended family

A ▶ **2.2** Look at the family tree. Complete the sentences using the words in the box. Listen and check your answers.

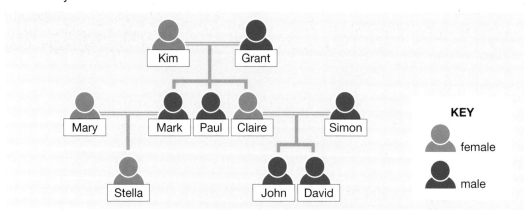

KEY

🟥 female

⬛ male

brother-in-law	cousin	grandchild	grandfather
mother-in-law	nephew	niece	son-in-law

1 Kim is Mary's _____ .

2 Stella is John's _____ .

3 Grant is John's _____ .

4 Simon is Kim's _____ .

5 John is Grant's _____ .

6 Simon is Paul's _____ .

7 Stella is Claire's _____ .

8 David is Mark's _____ .

B Work with a partner. Describe a connection to someone in your family. Your partner must name the relationship.

> Joanna is my mother's father's mother.

> Is she your great-grandmother?

LISTENING My family history

> **Listening for contractions versus possessives**
> When we hear "**'s**" after a noun of a person's name, it might be a contraction of *is* or a possessive form. Listen carefully to be sure you catch the right meaning.
> **Contraction of *is*:** *John's 21 years old.*
> **Possessive form:** *John's cousin is 21 years old.*

A ▶ **2.3** Watch Ken Lejtenyi talking about his family history. Circle the countries that he mentions.

Canada	England	France	Hungary
Italy	Romania	Scotland	Singapore

B ▶ **2.3** Watch again. Complete the sentences with a country from **A**.

1 Lejtenyi's mother's parents moved to Canada from _____.

2 His mother was born in _____.

3 His father's parents met in _____.

4 His father grew up in _____.

C CRITICAL THINKING

Reflecting Do you think many Canadians have an international family history like Lejtenyi? Discuss with a partner.

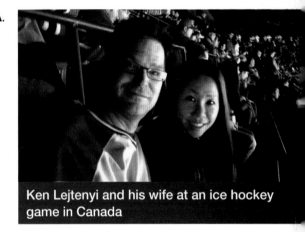

Ken Lejtenyi and his wife at an ice hockey game in Canada

SPEAKING Talking about family

A ▶ **2.4** Where are they going to hold the family reunion? Why?

A: What are you doing for the Lunar New Year?

B: Not much. How about you? Do you have any plans?   What are you doing? / What are your plans?

A: I'm going to spend it with my family. Every year, we have a family reunion.   get-together / gathering

B: That sounds fun. Do you have a big family?

A: Yeah. My mother has seven siblings, so I have more than twenty cousins.

B: Wow! Are they all coming to your place?   house / apartment

A: Oh, no. We're going to a restaurant. Our house is way too small.   much / far

B: Well, have a good time.

B Practice the conversation with a partner. Practice again using the words on the right.

C How many people are in your immediate family? How many are in your extended family? Tell a partner.

> There are five people in my immediate family—my parents, my two sisters, and me.

2B Generations

LANGUAGE FOCUS Discussing plans and arrangements

A ▶ **2.5** Read the information. Which record do you find the most amazing?

FAMILY RECORDS

The most generations alive in a single family has been seven. At 109, Augusta Bunge from the United States was the youngest living great-great-great-great-grandparent.

The highest number of children born to one mother is 69. The wife of Feodor Vassilyev from Russia (whose name is unknown) had 16 pairs of twins, seven sets of triplets, and four sets of quadruplets.

HAPPY BIRTHDAY

There is only one example of a family having five single children with the same birthday. Catherine (1952), Carol (1953), Charles (1956), Claudia (1961), and Cecilia Cummins (1966) were all born on 20th February.

B ▶ **2.6** Listen to someone telling his friend about some people he's going to meet this weekend. Circle the relationships.

a Chris is his (**first** / **second**) cousin.

b Emily is Chris's (**niece** / **daughter**).

C ▶ **2.7** Watch and study the language in the chart.

Talking about future plans	
I'm leaving for the reunion on Thursday. I'm not leaving on Friday.	
Are you going alone?	Yes, I am. / No, I'm not.
When are you coming back?	I'm coming back on Sunday.
I'm going to see my nephew this weekend. I'm not going to stay for very long.	
Are you going to meet your aunt and uncle?	Yes, I am. / No, I'm not.
What are you going to do afterwards?	I'm going to visit a few old friends.

For more information on **future forms**, see Grammar Summary 2 on page 155.

D ▶ **2.6** Circle the correct words to complete the sentences from the conversation in **B**.
Listen again to check your answers.

    1 "Are you (**do** / **doing**) anything interesting this weekend?"

    2 "I'm going to (**meet** / **meeting**) my second cousin."

    3 "He's (**bring** / **bringing**) his daughter."

    4 "I'm going to (**ask** / **asking**) Chris to help me find out more."

    5 "Where are you (**meet** / **meeting**) them?"

E Unscramble the questions. Then ask and answer them with a partner.

    1 this weekend / seeing / are / your grandparents / you

    _____?

    2 is going / which family member / to visit you / next

    _____?

    3 with your family / spending / you / are / your next vacation

    _____?

    4 you / anyone in your family / speaking with / are / this evening

    _____?

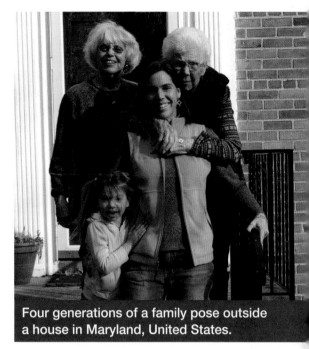

Four generations of a family pose outside a house in Maryland, United States.

F ▶ **2.8** Read the paragraph. Find and correct four mistakes. Listen and check your answers.

After I finish university, I going to take a year out. I think I need a break before I start working.
I'm going to travel around South America with my best friend Maki. We're meet this weekend
to work out our plans. We're definitely going to start in Argentina, but we haven't decided
where we're go after that. We don't have so much money so we're mainly going stay in
hostels. I can't wait. It's going to be a great adventure.

SPEAKING My family

A Walk around the room and find a different person who answers *yes* to each question. For each *yes*
answer, ask a follow-up question. Take notes.

Find someone who …	Name	Extra information
is going to call a family member later today.		
is meeting a family member this weekend.		
is going on a family vacation soon.		
has both a niece and a nephew.		
is going to a wedding soon.		
has three or more siblings.		

Are you going to call a family member later today?

Yes, I am. I'm going to call my parents.

B Share the most interesting information with the class.

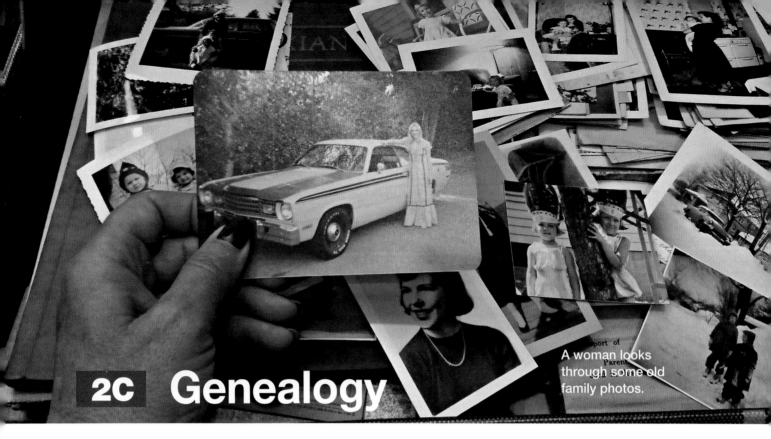

A woman looks through some old family photos.

2C Genealogy

PRE-READING Scanning

Work with a partner. Think of some reasons why people might search for information on their family history. Discuss your ideas. Then scan the passage to see if your ideas are mentioned.

▶ 2.9

1   Genealogy, the study of family history, is certainly nothing new. Family trees have been used for thousands of years to demonstrate claims to **wealth** and power. But the rise of the Internet has given the pursuit an explosion of new life.

2   According to some sources, genealogy is now one of the most popular topics on the Internet. Modern genealogists have a huge amount of information available online, and are able to connect with people from all around the world **with ease**. One popular ancestry website provides access to approximately 16 billion historical records. Its two million subscribers[1] have added 200 million photographs, documents, and stories to connect with 70 million family trees.

3   But what's behind our motivation to find out about our **ancestors**? Some people may have specific reasons. **Tracing** your family tree may help you reconnect with lost relatives. **Adopted** children can find out more about their birth parents. Others may want to discover a connection to a historical figure. Perhaps the most common motivation, though, is simply curiosity—a desire to better understand our place in the world. Genealogy can show our connections with people from entirely different backgrounds. As Helen Keller[2] once said, "There is no king who has not had a slave[3] among his ancestors, and no slave who has not had a king among his."

4   A. J. Jacobs's interest in genealogy started when he received an email from his twelfth cousin. Since then, Jacobs has joined one of the world's biggest family trees on Geni.com, which includes more than 75 million people. Jacobs believes that if we all realized that we're connected in this way, a lot of the problems in the world could be solved. As Jacobs says, "We're not just part of the same species. We're part of the same family."

---

[1] **subscriber:** *n.* someone who pays to get access to a website or to receive copies of a newspaper or magazine

[2] **Helen Keller:** *n.* an American writer, educator, and activist who was both blind and deaf

[3] **slave:** *n.* a person who is the legal property of another person

UNDERSTANDING PURPOSE

Read the passage. What is the main purpose?

   a to explain the history of genealogy

   b to teach the reader how to research their family tree

   c to explain why people are interested in genealogy

UNDERSTANDING MAIN IDEAS

Match each paragraph to its main idea.

   1 Paragraph 1   ○   ○   People search for their ancestors for a variety of reasons.

   2 Paragraph 2   ○   ○   Genealogy could help solve problems in the world.

   3 Paragraph 3   ○   ○   Genealogy is very popular on the Internet.

   4 Paragraph 4   ○   ○   Genealogy is not new, but the Internet is changing it.

UNDERSTANDING DETAILS

Answer the questions. Circle the correct option.

   1 What proof is given that genealogy is popular on the Internet?

      a the number of Internet searches

      b statistics from an ancestry website

   2 Which of these is given as a reason for an interest in genealogy?

      a to see if an ancestor had a medical condition

      b to find lost family members

   3 What does Helen Keller's quote mean?

      a Everyone is connected to people from different backgrounds.

      b People often use genealogy to show a connection to rich people.

   4 Why did A. J. Jacobs become interested in genealogy?

      a He found out he was related to a famous person.

      b A distant relative contacted him.

BUILDING VOCABULARY

A Match each word in **blue** from the passage to its definition.

   1 wealth   ○   ○   possession of a large amount of valuable things

   2 with ease   ○   ○   to find or discover

   3 ancestors   ○   ○   legally raised as your own child

   4 trace   ○   ○   people in your family from past times

   5 adopted   ○   ○   without difficulty

B CRITICAL THINKING

   Applying To find out more about your family history, who would you talk to first? What questions would you ask? Discuss with a partner.

The world's largest family reunion

TEDTALKS

Writer **A. J. JACOBS** finds genealogy **fascinating**. After receiving an email from a man who claimed to be his twelfth cousin, Jacobs began planning a huge **family reunion** to meet his extended family. His idea worth spreading is that studying the world's "family tree" helps scientific progress, highlights our equality, and connects us to our **shared history** and to one another.

PREVIEWING

Read the paragraph above. Circle the correct option for each sentence below. You will hear these words in the TED Talk.

1 Something that is **fascinating** is extremely (**interesting** / **well-known**).

2 A **family reunion** is a (**gathering** / **written list**) of family members.

3 If you have **shared history** with someone, you have (**a common background** / **famous ancestors**).

VIEWING

A ▶ **2.10** Watch Part 1 of the TED Talk. Check [✓] the points Jacobs makes.

☐ Genealogy is undergoing a revolution partly because of genetics and the Internet.

☐ People can add their own information online to create and combine huge family trees.

☐ Putting our personal family information online can be a dangerous thing to do.

☐ Most people have famous people and historical figures in their family trees.

B ▶ **2.11** Watch Part 2 of the TED Talk. Jacobs gives four reasons why a world family tree is a good idea. Match each idea to a supporting detail.

Main ideas	Supporting details
1 It has scientific value. ○	○ We all come from the same ancestor.
2 It brings history alive. ○	○ We treat family better than we treat strangers.
3 It shows we are all connected. ○	○ Jacobs found out he was related to a famous person.
4 It creates a kinder world. ○	○ It provides a better understanding of human migration.

C ▶ **2.12** Watch Part 3 of the TED Talk. Complete the notes.

Event   The biggest _____ in history

Activities   Exhibits, _____, _____, a day of _____

Who's invited? _____

D CRITICAL THINKING

Evaluating Look back at **C**. Why do you think Jacobs wants to hold this event? Would you like to attend? Discuss with a partner.

VOCABULARY IN CONTEXT

▶ **2.13** Watch the excerpts from the TED Talk. Choose the correct meaning of the words.

PRESENTATION SKILLS Personalizing a presentation

Some speakers choose to include personal information in their presentations. Including stories about yourself, or your family members, can help engage your audience and make your presentation more "real."

A ▶ **2.14** Watch the excerpt. What does Jacobs do to personalize the presentation?

   a He talks about his uncle.

   b He shows a photo of a family member.

   c He tells a personal story.

B Jacobs personalizes his presentation in other ways. Match the phrases below.
▶ **2.15** Watch the excerpts to check your answer.

1 "[Genealogy] brings history alive."   ○   ○   "I have three sons, so I see how they fight."

2 "Now, I know there are family feuds."   ○   ○   "Here's my cousin Gwyneth Paltrow. She has no idea I exist, but we are officially cousins."

3 "So that's 75 million people connected by blood or marriage."   ○   ○   "I found out I'm connected to Albert Einstein, so I told my seven-year-old son that, and he was totally engaged."

C Work with a partner. Imagine you are giving a talk on the topics below. How could you use personalization?

| the cost of living | climate change | an endangered animal |

A. J. Jacobs at the Global Family Reunion

I AM A COUSIN

2E One big happy family

COMMUNICATE Family tree

A Work in a group of four. You are going to work together to draw a family tree.
Student A: Turn to page 141. **Student B**: Turn to page 142.
Student C: Turn to page 144. **Student D**: Turn to page 146.

B Read out pieces of information and ask each other questions to find how everyone is related to each other. Complete the family tree on page 147.

Alice is Steve's wife.

OK. Do they have any children?

Yes, they have a daughter called ...

Steve   Alice

?   ?

> ### Checking information
> *John is ..., isn't he?*   *So you said that ... ?*
> *Are you saying that they're ....?*   *Let me just check something, did you say ...?*

WRITING An invitation

You are organizing a reunion for your family. Decide when, where, and how long it's going to be. Write a group email to your family members telling them the details.

> Hi everyone!
>
> I have great news! I am currently organizing a family reunion, and you're all invited! It's going to take place next July 22–23 during the summer break. It's only going to be two days, but you can stay longer if you like. It's going to be at ...

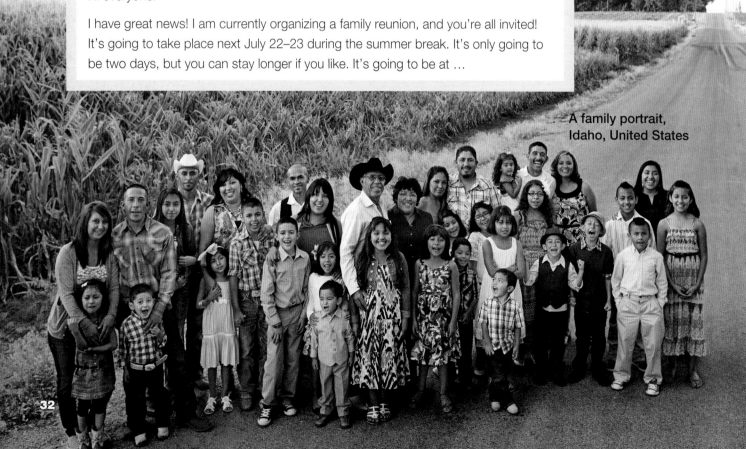

A family portrait, Idaho, United States

32

3 Global Stories

TED

"It's often said that you can tell a lot about a person by looking at what's on their bookshelves. "

Ann Morgan
Writer, TED speaker

UNIT GOALS

In this unit, you will …

- talk about popular books.
- read reviews of several books from around the world.
- watch a TED Talk about an unusual reading goal.

WARM UP

▶ **3.1** Watch part of Ann Morgan's TED Talk. Answer the questions with a partner.

1 Do you agree with the quote above?

2 What do your bookshelves say about you?

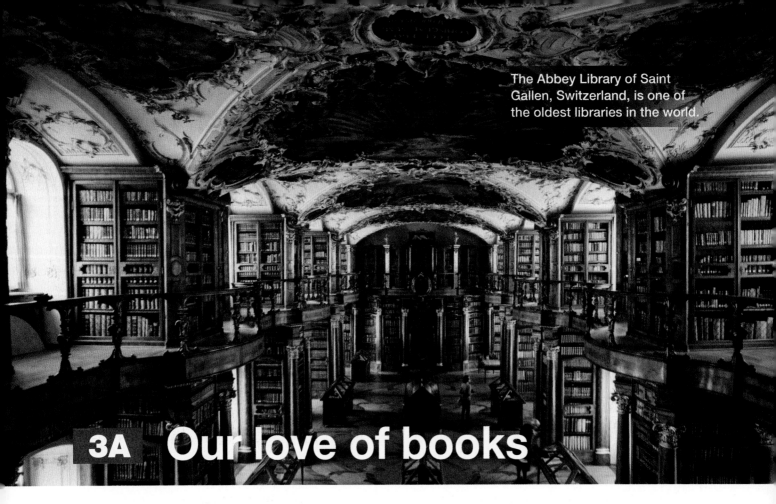

The Abbey Library of Saint Gallen, Switzerland, is one of the oldest libraries in the world.

3A Our love of books

VOCABULARY Genres of fiction

A ▶ 3.2 Match each genre of fiction to its definition. Listen and check your answers.

1	A fairy tale	○	○	is based on characters from a book, movie, or TV show.
2	A horror story	○	○	creates fear in the reader.
3	Fan fiction	○	○	often includes magical creatures and is usually for children.

4	A graphic novel	○	○	has a fictional story and is set in the past.
5	Historical fiction	○	○	is drawn like a comic strip.
6	A fantasy story	○	○	is usually set in an imaginary, magical world.

7	A romance novel	○	○	is an exciting fictional story that is often about crime.
8	A thriller	○	○	tells a love story.
9	A sci-fi (science-fiction) story	○	○	takes place in the future, often in space.

B Work with a partner. Which genres do you enjoy? Can you think of an example of a book for each one?

C Look at these elements of a story. Then briefly describe one book you have read to your partner.

Characters: who the story is about

Setting: where and when the story takes place

Plot: what happens in the story

Theme: the central idea of the story

LISTENING Interview with an author

A ▶ **3.3** Madeleine Thien is an author. Watch and circle **T** for true or **F** for false.

Madeleine Thien

1 As a child, Thien knew she wanted to be an author. **T** **F**

2 Thien's first book was a collection of short stories. **T** **F**

3 Thien has published three books in total. **T** **F**

> **Taking notes while listening**
> When you listen and take notes at the same time, don't write down everything you hear. Be selective and write down only the key words and phrases.

B ▶ **3.3** Watch and complete the chart about the story she describes.

Setting	Characters	Story

C CRITICAL THINKING

Reflecting Do you think you'd enjoy this book? Why or why not? Discuss with a partner.

SPEAKING Talking about books

A ▶ **3.4** What's the book about?

A: What are you reading?

B: Oh, it's a book called *And Then There Were None.* Do you know it?

A: No, I don't think so. What kind of book is it? A horror story?   fantasy story / fairy tale

B: No, it's a mystery. It's about a group of people   It's a story about / It tells the story of who are stuck on an island together.

A: It sounds cool. Is it any good?   worth reading / interesting

B: Yeah, I can't put it down.

A: Wow! Can I borrow it when you've finished?   you're done / you've read it

B: Sure. I think you'll like it.

B Practice the conversation with a partner. Practice again using the words on the right.

C Work with a partner. What's your favorite book? Explain what it's about.

> My favorite book is *Hyperion* by Dan Simmons. It's a science fiction story about six unique characters who visit the planet Hyperion.

3B What's it about?

LANGUAGE FOCUS Describing stories

A ▶ **3.5** Read the information. Which of these books do you know?

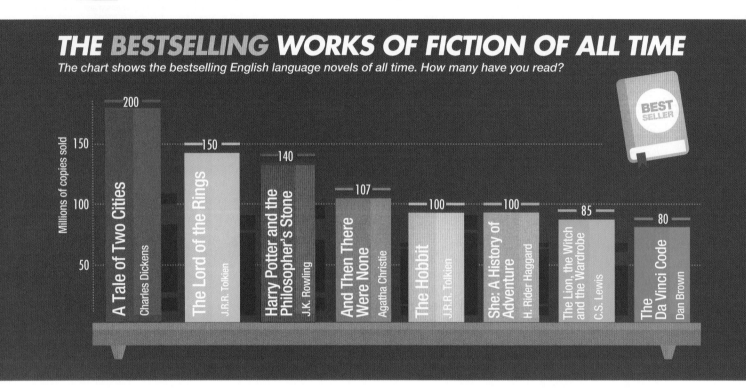

THE BESTSELLING WORKS OF FICTION OF ALL TIME

The chart shows the bestselling English language novels of all time. How many have you read?

Millions of copies sold

- A Tale of Two Cities — Charles Dickens — 200
- The Lord of the Rings — J.R.R. Tolkien — 150
- Harry Potter and the Philosopher's Stone — J.K. Rowling — 140
- And There Were None — Agatha Christie — 107
- The Hobbit — J.R.R. Tolkien — 100
- She: A History of Adventure — H. Rider Haggard — 100
- The Lion, the Witch and the Wardrobe — C.S. Lewis — 85
- The Da Vinci Code — Dan Brown — 80

BEST SELLER

B ▶ **3.6** Listen to two people talk about one of the books. Complete the sentences.

The Lion, the Witch, and the Wardrobe is a ¹_____ novel about four ²_____ who live in an old house. They go through a magical wardrobe and visit a place called Narnia. Narnia is a place where ³_____ can talk.

C ▶ **3.7** Watch and study the language in the chart.

Adding details to people, things, and places
People
And Then There Were None is about a group of people who are stuck on an island.
One of the characters is a young man who is rich and handsome.
Things
The Da Vinci Code is a mystery novel that has sold millions of copies worldwide.
A Tale of Two Cities is a piece of historical fiction that is set in London and Paris.
Places
Narnia is a magical place where animals can talk.

For more information on **relative clauses**, see Grammar Summary 3 on page 155.

D Match the two parts of each sentence.

1 *The Hobbit* is a fantasy book ○ ○ where two adventurers meet a mysterious queen.

2 *The Da Vinci Code* is about two people ○ ○ who studies magic at school.

3 The Harry Potter books are stories ○ ○ who investigate a murder in Paris.

4 Harry Potter is a wizard ○ ○ that takes place in Middle Earth.

5 *She* is set in a lost African kingdom ○ ○ that are popular with kids and adults.

E ▶ **3.8** Find and correct three mistakes. Listen and check your answers.

The Alchemist, by Brazilian novelist Paulo Coelho, is a story about a shepherd boy where travels from Spain to Morocco. He eventually goes to a place in Egypt, looking for treasure that might be buried there. Along the way, he meets people who teaches him many life lessons. It's a story who is both charming and dramatic. I would recommend this book to anyone who wants to read a nice story about becoming who you want to be.

F Complete the sentences with your own ideas. Then compare with a partner.

1 I like stories that _____ .

2 I like authors who _____ .

3 I don't enjoy books that _____ .

4 My favorite book has a character who _____ .

SPEAKING Can you guess?

A Work alone. Think of a famous book or story. Write three sentences to describe the book in the table below.

	A famous book or story
1	
2	
3	

B Work with a partner. Take turns reading out one of your sentences. After each sentence, try to guess the name of the book.

This is a very famous novel which is set in Russia.

Sorry, I don't know. Give me another clue.

It's about a man who commits a horrible crime.

3C Top picks

Skim the text. Why did Ann Morgan like each book?

▶ **3.9** Writer and blogger Ann Morgan loves to share her passion for books. Here are three books she highly recommends.

Lake Como by Srdjan Valjarević

This very funny book follows a Serbian writer named Frank who receives a scholarship[1] and moves to Italy to write. But he doesn't do any work. Instead, he spends his days chatting, watching TV, and sleeping. Frank doesn't write his book, but the connections he makes with the local people take on more importance. The book is about those connections, as well as the meaning of culture and **identity**.

Ann Morgan found it "a great read" and says it "has that rare gift of revealing how people can grow and learn from one another."

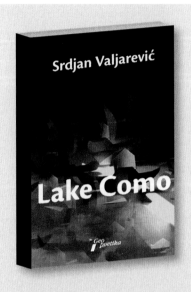

Crowfall by Shanta Gokhale

Crowfall is a big, **ambitious** book. The story follows a group of characters who are just starting their careers in Mumbai, India—three painters, a musician, a journalist, and a teacher. The book highlights some **revealing** things about art and music, but is mainly about loss. Throughout the story, there are several deaths that occur, and a loved one goes missing.

Morgan called this book "a **marvelous** read," and especially loved the author's clear, powerful language.

The Blue Sky by Galsan Tschinag

The Blue Sky is a coming-of-age story[2] about a young boy named Dshurukuwaa who lives in Mongolia's Altai Mountains. It's a world that is changing. All around Dshurukuwaa, the traditions of his ancestors are crumbling under the pressures of modern life. In the novel, we get a fascinating **glimpse** into a way of living that is disappearing quickly.

This was one of Morgan's favorite books. She wrote in her blog that it was "impossible not to feel connected to and invested in this world."

---

[1] **scholarship:** *n.* a sum of money meant to support a student's education

[2] **coming-of-age story:** *n.* a story that focuses on a character's growth from youth to adulthood

UNDERSTANDING DETAILS

A What is the plot of each story? Match the two parts of each sentence.

1 *Lake Como* is about ○   ○ a group of people and the losses some of them experience.

2 *Crowfall* is about ○   ○ a boy and the changes that are happening in his culture.

3 *The Blue Sky* is about ○   ○ a writer who makes meaningful connections with people.

B Complete the chart.

Title	Setting	Characters	Theme
Lake Como			
Crowfall			
The Blue Sky			

MAKING INFERENCES

Which comment do you think probably belongs to each book? Match.

1 *Lake Como* ○   ○ "It's sad that customs from the past are no longer practiced today."

2 *Crowfall* ○   ○ "It made me think a lot about my grandmother. She died last year."

3 *The Blue Sky* ○   ○ "I couldn't put it down I was laughing so hard."

BUILDING VOCABULARY

A Match each word in **blue** from the passage to its definition.

1 **identity** ○   ○ giving information

2 **ambitious** ○   ○ extremely good

3 **revealing** ○   ○ the beliefs and qualities of a person

4 **glimpse** ○   ○ wanting to be successful

5 **marvelous** ○   ○ a quick look

B CRITICAL THINKING

Evaluating Which book would you prefer to read? Why? Discuss with a partner.

3D My year reading a book from every country

TEDTALKS

ANN MORGAN made an **alarming** discovery several years ago when she looked at her bookshelves and saw how **narrow** her reading focus was. Her idea worth spreading is that stories from other countries and cultures have **extraordinary** power to introduce new values and ideas, and to show us our own **blind spots**.

PREVIEWING

Read the paragraph above. Match each **bold** word to its meaning.
You will hear these words in the TED Talk.

1 limited: _____

2 frightening: _____

3 impressive; remarkable: _____

4 things you aren't aware of: _____

VIEWING

A ▶ **3.10** Watch Part 1 of the TED Talk. Answer the questions.

1 What did Morgan discover about her bookshelf?

   a Most of the books she owned were the same genre.

   b Most of her books were by American or British authors.

   c Most of the books she owned were set in England.

2 What goal did Morgan set for herself?

   a She would read one book from a different country every year.

   b She would read a book from every country in a year.

   c She would start to translate books from other countries.

B ▶ **3.11** Watch Part 2 of the TED Talk. Number the events in the order they happened from 1 to 5.

_____ Strangers began to offer suggestions.

_____ Morgan asked for book suggestions.

_____ Friends and family began to offer suggestions.

___1___ Morgan registered her blog.

_____ Morgan received two books from someone in Malaysia.

C ▶ **3.11** Watch Part 2 of the TED Talk again. What surprised Morgan about the response to her project? Discuss with a partner.

D ▷ **3.12** Watch Part 3 of the TED Talk. What did Morgan learn from her experience? Check [✓] the statements that she would agree with.

☐ You see the world in a different way.

☐ The countries that you read about begin to feel more real.

☐ You can get a rounded picture of a country by reading a book.

☐ Books have the power to connect people.

E   CRITICAL THINKING

Applying Morgan's project opened her eyes to new ideas and experiences. What other projects could someone do to achieve the same goal?

VOCABULARY IN CONTEXT

▷ **3.13** Watch the excerpts from the TED Talk. Choose the correct meaning of the words.

PRESENTATION SKILLS Closing a presentation

> One way to close a presentation is to ask the audience to join you in supporting or acting on something. Here are other ways to close a presentation.
>
> *Summarize your main points.*   *Show a powerful visual.*
> *Give an inspiring quote.*   *Circle back to the opener.*
> *Add a personal story.*   *Describe your hope for the future.*

A ▷ **3.14** Watch part of Morgan's TED Talk. How does she end her presentation?

a   She shows a powerful visual.

b   She gives a quote from an author.

c   She talks about her hopes for the future.

B ▷ **3.15** Now watch TED speaker Munir Virani. Check [✓] the ways he closes his presentation.

☐ He shows powerful visuals.   ☐ He shares a personal story.

☐ He gives a call to action.   ☐ He asks the audience a question.

C   Work in a group. Whose closing do you think is more effective—Virani's or Morgan's? Why?

3E A good read

COMMUNICATE A book recommendation

A Work in a group. Brainstorm a list of books from your country. Include books from a variety of genres, such as novels, autobiographies, children's stories, and fiction.

B Imagine that Ann Morgan asked you for a suggestion on a book to read from your country. Agree on one book and list two reasons why it's a good choice.

> Book title:
>
> Author: Genre:
>
> What it's about:
>
> Reason 1:
>
> Reason 2:

In your opinion, which book best represents our country?

I think we should suggest …

Asking for opinions
Which do you think …?   In your opinion, what's …?   What do you feel is …?

C Take turns presenting your book suggestions. Answer any questions from the class.

WRITING Book review

A Write a short review about a book you read. Include the title, author, and information about the setting, characters, and plot.

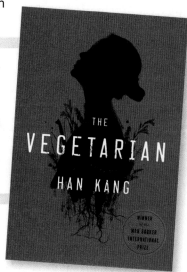

A strange but interesting story   ★★★★

I recently read *The Vegetarian* by Korean writer Han Kang. The story takes place in South Korea. The main characters are Yeong-hye and her husband, Mr. Cheong. It's about a wife who doesn't want to follow society's rules. After she has a frightening dream, she decides to become a vegetarian.

B Work in a group. Read each other's reviews. In your opinion, which book sounds the most interesting? Why?

Presentation 1

MODEL PRESENTATION

A Complete the transcript of the presentation using the words in the box.

cousin	endangered	facing	going to	help
reptile	that	traveling	where	work

I'd like to talk to you about an amazing ¹_____ that really needs our help—the sea turtle. Last month, I went diving off the coast of Mozambique in Africa with my ²_____, Maria. I saw so many amazing things, but the animal ³_____ I remember more than any others was this beautiful loggerhead sea turtle. My dive instructor told me how lucky I was. He said that sea turtles were ⁴_____ and seeing one wasn't so common any more. I later found out that many turtles are killed by humans for their eggs, meat, skin, and shells. The turtles' habitats and the coastal areas ⁵_____ they lay their eggs are also under threat. So, how can you ⁶_____? Well, firstly, when you're ⁷_____, be careful what you buy. Ask questions if you think a souvenir might be made from a turtle shell. Secondly, support a turtle charity. There are many organizations that ⁸_____ to help save sea turtles. I'm now a member of a sea turtle charity and next month I'm ⁹_____ take part in a fundraising event. Finally, you can spread the word. Tell other people about these animals and the dangers they are ¹⁰_____.

Thank you so much.

B ▶ **P.1** Watch the presentation and check your answers.

C ▶ **P.1** Review the list of presentation skills from Units 1–3 below. Which does the speaker use? Check [✓] each skill used as you watch again.

The speaker …
- ☐ uses questions to signpost
- ☐ personalizes the presentation
- ☐ closes the presentation effectively

D Look at the notes the speaker made before her presentation. Did she forget to say anything?

- Introduction: amazing reptile / sea turtle
- Trip to Mozambique / diving
- Dive instructor / lucky / endangered
- Turtles killed for eggs/meat, etc. / habitat threatened
- How can you help?
- Careful what you buy and eat when abroad
- Support a charity / spread the word

YOUR TURN

A You are going to plan and give a short presentation to a partner introducing an endangered animal. Use the notes above for ideas and research any other information. Make notes on a card or a small piece of paper.

B Look at the useful phrases in the box below. Think about which ones you will need in your presentation.

> **Useful phrases**
>
> | | |
> |---|---|
> | **Introducing your topic:** | *I'd like to (tell you / talk to you) about …* |
> | **Types of animals:** | *amphibians, birds, fish, insects, mammals, reptiles* |
> | **Describing conservation status:** | *threatened, vulnerable, (critically) endangered, extinct* |
> | **Signposting questions:** | *Why do they need our help? / How can you help?* |
> | **Ending:** | *Thank you so much (for listening).* |
> | | *Thanks for listening.* |

C Work with a partner. Take turns giving your presentation using your notes. Use some of the presentation skills from Units 1–3. As you listen, check [✓] each skill your partner uses.

The speaker …
- ☐ uses questions to signpost
- ☐ personalizes the presentation
- ☐ closes the presentation effectively

D Give your partner some feedback on their talk. Include two things you liked, and one thing he or she can improve.

> Well done! You spoke really clearly and I loved the way you personalized the presentation. Next time, try to make more eye contact with your audience.

4 Music

" Recently, I flew over a
crowd of thousands of people
in Brazil, playing music by
George Frideric Handel. "

Daria van den Bercken
Pianist, TED speaker

UNIT GOALS

In this unit, you will ...

• talk about how music affects us.

• read about why music makes us feel good.

• watch a TED Talk by a musician who gives unusual
concerts.

WARM UP

▶ **4.1** Watch part of Daria van den Bercken's TED
Talk. Answer the questions with a partner.

1 What kind of music does van den Bercken play?

2 Do you like this kind of music?

Fans reach out to touch their music idol.

4A Feel the music

VOCABULARY Music

A ▶ **4.2** Listen and number the musical genres from 1 to 6 in the order you hear them.

_____ classical

_____ country

_____ electronic

_____ easy listening

_____ heavy metal

_____ hip-hop

B Complete the chart with words from the box.

energized	loud	soothing	relaxed	soft	sleepy

Words to describe music		How music makes you feel	
dark	_____	nostalgic	_____
upbeat	_____	melancholic	_____
rhythmic	_____	romantic	_____

C ▶ **4.2** Listen again to the music from **A**. Work with a partner. Describe each piece of music.

The easy listening music is very soft.

Yeah, it makes me feel very relaxed.

LISTENING A traditional singer

Iarla Ó Lionáird
performing live

> **Understanding accents**
> At first, an unfamiliar accent can be difficult to understand. Try to identify the vowel sounds that are different and listen to other examples of the same accent to increase your familiarity with it.

A **4.3** Iarla Ó Lionáird is a musician who sings in a style called *sean-nós*. Watch the video. Which country does sean-nós singing come from?

B **4.3** Watch again. Circle **T** for True or **F** for False.

1 Ó Lionáird sings in English.	**T**	**F**
2 Some of his relatives were also singers.	**T**	**F**
3 Ó Lionáird's teacher, Mrs. McSweeney, encouraged him to sing.	**T**	**F**
4 Ó Lionáird released his first solo album in 2014.	**T**	**F**

C CRITICAL THINKING

Personalizing What words would you use to describe Ó Lionáird's music? How does the music make you feel? Discuss with a partner

SPEAKING Talking about music

A **4.4** What kind of music is the man listening to?

A: What are you listening to?

B: Oh, it's a band called *The National*. Here, listen.

A: Hey, they're pretty good. I've never heard them before.

B: Yeah, they're not so famous, but they've been around a while. They've done a lot of albums.   well-known / popular   made / produced

A: This song's great. I love this kind of melancholic rock.

B: Me too. But they have a few really loud, upbeat songs, too. Here, listen to this one.   some / one or two

A: Wow! I see what you mean. Do you have many of their albums?

B: I have them all. And they have a concert here in July. I can't wait.   gig / show

B Practice the conversation with a partner. Practice again using the words on the right.

C Work with a partner. Tell each other about a band or singer that you like. Explain why.

> I really like Norah Jones. She has some really romantic songs, and she has such a good voice.

> Yeah, me too. I have a few of her albums.

4B Just the right music

LANGUAGE FOCUS Discussing types of music

A ▶ **4.5** Read the information. When should you listen to classical music?

WHAT'S THE BEST MUSIC FOR ...?

STUDYING
Best music: classical or instrumental music
Examples: Mozart's sonatas or Spanish guitar
Why? It makes it easier for you to concentrate and take in new information.

GETTING TO SLEEP
Best music: soft classical music
Examples: the works of Handel and Bach
Why? It slows down brainwaves and helps you relax.

EXERCISING
Best music: electronic, hip-hop, or pop songs
Examples: Lady Gaga's *Applause*
Why? It has a fast and regular rhythm.

DRIVING
Best music: pop songs with a gentle tempo
Examples: Justin Timberlake's *Cry Me a River*
Why? The rhythm matches your heartbeat and keeps you calm so you drive carefully.

B ▶ **4.6** Listen to a music expert talk about the best music to listen to while studying. Circle the correct words to complete the recommendations.

1 Listen to songs (**with** / **without**) words.

2 Listen to (**the radio** / **your favorite album**).

C ▶ **4.7** Watch and study the language in the chart.

Talking about quantity	
Things you can count	***Things you cannot count***
I like this song. these songs.	I like this music.
There were too many people.	There was too much noise.
Do you have many songs on your phone? I have a lot of pop songs. I don't have many country songs.	Do you have much music on your phone? I have a lot of pop music. I don't have much country music.
How many people were at the concert? There were a lot / many. There were only a few.	How much traffic was there? There was a lot. There was only a little.

For more information on **countable and uncountable nouns**, see Grammar Extension 4 on page 156.

D Circle the correct words.

1 A: Do you like (**this music** / **these music**)?

  B: I do. Do you know where I can download some (**song** / **songs**)?

2 A: Did it take (**many** / **much**) time to download that new song?

  B: Yeah. I think too (**many** / **much**) people were trying to download it at once.

3 A: (**Were** / **Was**) there a big crowd at the concert?

  B: Not really. There were only a (**few** / **little**) people.

E Correct the mistake in each sentence.

1 I love this band but they don't do many live concert these days.

2 The performer stopped because there was too many noise coming from the crowd.

3 I was amazed by how few equipment the band had on stage.

4 After the band finished their last song, there were a lot of applause.

F ▶ **4.8** Complete the information. Circle the correct words. Listen and check your answers.

If you're a student who's struggling with too
¹(**many** / **much**) exams, a ²(**few** / **little**) classical
music might just help. According to ³(**many** / **much**)
different academic studies, classical music has
⁴(**many** / **much**) benefits for your brain and body that
can make a difference at exam time. It's been shown
that listening to classical music has an effect on how
⁵(**many** / **much**) new information you can learn. And if
you're stressed or not getting ⁶(**many** / **much**) sleep,
classical music can help, too. It can help you relax, and
is also said to reduce blood pressure.

SPEAKING Musical preferences

A Interview your partner. Take notes.

What's the best music for …?	Music
getting to sleep	
when you feel sad	
a party	
studying late at night	
a long-distance drive	
a romantic dinner	

What do you think is the best music for relaxing?

I think jazz is the best. It's very soothing.

B Work in a group. Share the most interesting information you heard.

A woman plays the violin during an orchestral performance.

4C Music and the brain

PRE-READING Previewing

▶ **4.9** Listen to part of Johannes Brahms' Hungarian Dance No. 5. How does it make you feel? Discuss with a partner.

▶ **4.10**

1 One day several years ago, Valorie Salimpoor took a drive that changed her life. Salimpoor, a neuroscience[1] graduate, was struggling to decide on her career path. She felt that a drive might help clear her head. When she **turned on** the car radio, a piece of violin music came on: Brahms' Hungarian Dance No. 5. "Something just happened," she recalls. "I just felt this rush of emotion ... It was so intense." She stopped the car so she could focus on the music. She wondered why it had such a powerful **effect** on her.

2 Salimpoor found a job working as a neuroscientist. Her **research** involved scanning people's brain activity as they listened to music. She discovered that when people listen to music they like, their brains flood with dopamine—a **chemical** linked with pleasure and motivation. In one experiment, people listened to the first 30 seconds of unfamiliar songs. The listeners were then given the option of buying the full songs, using their own money. By analyzing dopamine-related areas of the participants' brains, Salimpoor was able to successfully predict which songs the people

would choose to buy; she could tell what they liked and what they didn't based on brain activity.

3 But why might one person like a song while another person doesn't? Salimpoor says it all depends on past musical experiences. "Eastern, Western, jazz, heavy metal, pop—all of these have different rules they follow," she says. These rules are recorded as patterns, or templates, in the brain. If the new music has a familiar template, your brain releases dopamine and **registers** a feeling of pleasure. This might explain why most people have a preference for a certain type of music.

4 There are questions Salimpoor is still trying to answer: How does our brain make musical templates? Why do people with similar backgrounds have different preferences? Her research, though, has given her a new way to think about her experience years ago. "That day," she says, "it all seemed like such a big mystery." Now when she hears a piece of music she likes, she has a better understanding of what's happening inside her brain.

[1] **neuroscience:** *n.* the study of the brain and nervous system

UNDERSTANDING GIST

Read the passage. Which two questions does the passage discuss?

a Why does music affect our emotions?   **c** When did our brains first hear music?

b What is the happiest music to listen to?   **d** Why do different people like different kinds of music?

UNDERSTANDING DETAILS

Circle the best answer for each question.

1 Why was Hungarian Dance No. 5 special for Salimpoor?

    a It brought back a very happy memory.

    b It had a strong effect on her career.

    c It made her think of a favorite piece of music.

2 What is the main idea of Paragraph 2?

    a An experiment showed that classical music usually makes people happy.

    b Researchers found a link between music and chemical activity in the brain.

    c According to a study, certain types of music can slow down brain activity.

3 What are the "templates" referred to in Paragraph 3?

    a special tools that are used in brain scan experiments

    b types of music that have a very strong emotional impact

    c patterns in the brain that relate to certain types of music

4 The following sentence would be best placed at the end of which paragraph?

Right then, she decided her future career.

    a Paragraph 1   **b** Paragraph 2   **c** Paragraph 3

5 What does "mystery" in Paragraph 4 refer to?

    a where memory templates are stored in the brain

    b which part of the brain produces the most dopamine

    c what happens in our brains when we listen to music

BUILDING VOCABULARY

A Complete each sentence using the correct form of the words in **blue** from the passage.

1 A scientist usually has to do a lot of _____ as part of their job.

2 _____ released by our brains can effect our emotions.

3 The earthquake _____ 7.2 on the Richter scale.

4 You can _____ your TV with a remote control.

5 Certain songs can have an emotional _____ on people.

B CRITICAL THINKING

Applying What kinds of music have the greatest effect on you? Why do you think those types of music are special? Discuss with a partner.

4D Why I take the piano on the road ... and in the air

TEDTALKS

A few years ago, **DARIA VAN DEN BERCKEN** discovered George Handel's keyboard music. When she started to play it, she was in complete **awe**. What she experienced that day set her on a journey to share the beauty of music with others. Her idea worth spreading is that we should try to enjoy music the way a child does—full of **wonder** and with pure, **unprejudiced** amazement.

PREVIEWING

A Read the paragraph above. Circle the correct option for each sentence below. You will hear these words in the TED Talk.

1 If you are **in awe of** something, you (**admire** / **cannot appreciate**) it.

2 You are likely to be full of **wonder** (**on a beautiful mountain** / **in a dark room**).

3 When you are **unprejudiced**, you have (**an open** / **a closed**) mind about something.

B ▶ **4.11** Watch van den Bercken play two pieces of music. How do you think she describes each piece? Circle your ideas.

Piece 1: a melancholic   **b** relaxing   **Piece 2: a** energetic   **b** romantic

VIEWING

A ▶ **4.12** Watch Part 1 of the TED Talk. Circle the correct answers.

1 Why was van den Bercken surprised by the music she found on the Internet?

    a She didn't know Handel wrote keyboard music.   **b** It was extremely difficult to play.

2 Why was she "in awe" of the music?

    a because it was so difficult to play   **b** because it changed from sad to energetic

B ▶ **4.13** Watch Part 2 of the TED Talk. Who does van den Bercken describe when she makes these claims? Check [✓] the correct column.

	7- and 8-year-olds	11- and 12-year-olds
1 They're willing to listen to classical music.		
2 It's hard to get them to listen to classical music.		
3 The opinions of others matter to them.		
4 They listen to music without prejudice.		

C CRITICAL THINKING

Reflecting How have your musical tastes changed since you were a child? Discuss with a partner.

VOCABULARY IN CONTEXT

▶ **4.14** Watch the excerpts from the TED Talk. Choose the correct meaning of the words.

PRESENTATION SKILLS Providing background information

> During a presentation, it's often useful to include some information about your own background. This can help the audience understand why you're interested in the topic you're talking about.

A ▶ **4.15** Watch the excerpt. What background information does van den Bercken provide?

a who first got her interested in learning the piano

b how she learned something new about a composer

c the first time she heard someone play Handel's music

B ▶ **4.16** Now watch two other TED speakers. Match the speakers to the background information they give. One is extra.

1 A. J. Jacobs ○ ○ a a meeting with a famous person

2 Ann Morgan ○ ○ b an email that inspired them

○ c what they learned about themselves

C Work in a group. Think of something you are passionate about. Now imagine you are going to give a presentation about it. What background information about yourself would you provide?

" I fell in love with the music and I wanted to share it with as many people as possible. "

4E Musical choices

COMMUNICATE Desert island discs

A Imagine you are going to spend a year alone on a desert island. You can choose four songs to take with you and listen to while you're there. Write your list in the space below.

1 _____   3 _____

2 _____   4 _____

B Look at the questions below and prepare to answer them for each song on your list. Research any information you don't know.

Who wrote the song?	**What words would you use to describe the song?**
When was it written?	**Why is it important to you?**

C Work with a partner. Use the questions above to interview each other. Ask for extra information.

D Listen to each other's songs. Tell your partner your opinion.

Describing music
It makes me feel … It sounds … It reminds me of … When I listen to it, I …

WRITING A favorite song

Think of one more of your favorite songs. Explain how it makes you feel and why you like it. Does it have any special significance?

One of my favorite songs is *Wake Up* by Arcade Fire. I like it because it's a really powerful and energetic song, and it makes me feel happy. It reminds me of my time at university.

A man stands on a desert island in the Seychelles.

5 Good Design

" Trust me. One hundred percent of people care about flags. **"**

Roman Mars
Digital storyteller, TED speaker

UNIT GOALS

In this unit, you will …

- talk about design.
- read about the importance of city flags.
- watch a TED Talk about good flag design.

WARM UP

▶ **5.1** Watch part of Roman Mars's TED Talk. Answer the questions with a partner.

1 Describe a flag you know well.

2 Do you think it has a good design? Why or why not?

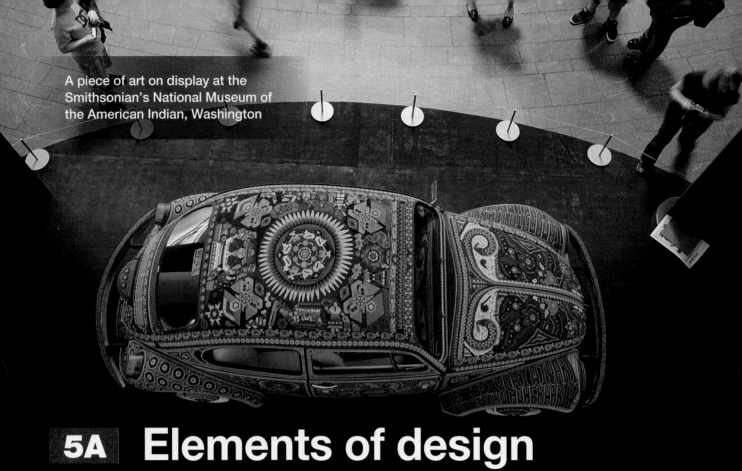

A piece of art on display at the Smithsonian's National Museum of the American Indian, Washington

5A Elements of design

VOCABULARY Design elements

A These words can be used to describe visual designs, including art. ~~Cross out~~ the word that does not belong in each category.

1 colors	bright	short	pale	vibrant	_____
2 lines	straight	happy	curved	thick	_____
3 shape	pale	round	triangular	square	_____
4 size	orange	tiny	large	huge	_____
5 texture	silky	empty	rough	smooth	_____
6 contrast	subtle	sharp	tall	dramatic	_____

B Work with a partner. Add one more word to each category.

C Work with a partner. Which of the words in **A** could be used to describe the art in the picture above?

D Do you like the art in the picture above? Why or why not? Discuss with a partner.

I like it. The colors are really vibrant.

Me too. I like the bright colors and the curved lines.

LISTENING A designer's advice

> **Identifying changes in topic**
> There are certain phrases in English that are used to signify a change in topic.
>
> *In regard to ...*   *As far as ... is concerned*   *Regarding ...*

Sarah Lafferty

A ▶ **5.2** Sarah Lafferty is an interior designer. Watch and complete the quote she gives.

"Have nothing in your houses that you do not know to be

_____ or believe to be _____."

William Morris, designer

B ▶ **5.2** Watch again. Circle the correct option to complete the sentences.

1 Lafferty's parents were (**architects** / **interior designers**).

2 Lafferty studied (**interior** / **textile**) design at university.

3 Lafferty wants the houses she designs to reflect her (**clients'** / **own**) tastes.

C CRITICAL THINKING

Applying Look again at the quote by William Morris. If you apply this idea to your own home, what would you need to change? Discuss with a partner.

SPEAKING Talking about design

A ▶ **5.3** Do you think the people will buy the sofa?

A: What do you think of this one?

B: This one? Don't you think the colors are a bit too bright?   strong / vibrant

A: No, I love the colors. And the shape is perfect for our living room.   ideal / just right

B: Yeah, but I don't think it will go with the rest of our furniture.   match / look good with

A: Why not?

B: All our other furniture is brown. This has yellow and pink stripes.

A: Our walls are yellow.

B: Yeah, but it's a very pale yellow. Can we look at something   light / soft
else, please?

B Practice the conversation with a partner. Practice again using the words on the right.

C Work with a partner. Turn to page 147. What do you like and dislike about each piece of furniture?

I like the shape and the colors.

I agree. But I think they're too bright.

5B Signs of the times

LANGUAGE FOCUS Discussing elements of design

A ▶ **5.4** Read the information. What were coats of arms originally for?

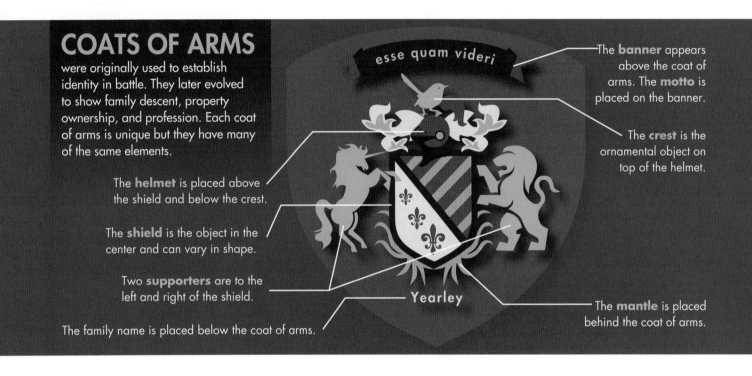

COATS OF ARMS were originally used to establish identity in battle. They later evolved to show family descent, property ownership, and profession. Each coat of arms is unique but they have many of the same elements.

The **helmet** is placed above the shield and below the crest.

The **shield** is the object in the center and can vary in shape.

Two **supporters** are to the left and right of the shield.

The family name is placed below the coat of arms.

esse quam videri

The **banner** appears above the coat of arms. The **motto** is placed on the banner.

The **crest** is the ornamental object on top of the helmet.

Yearley

The **mantle** is placed behind the coat of arms.

B ▶ **5.5** Listen to an expert explain the parts of a coat of arms. Circle the correct words.

1 (**All** / **Not all**) coats of arms have a motto.

2 Sometimes the motto is (**below** / **on**) the shield.

3 The two supporters are (**always** / **usually**) animals.

4 The shape of the shield (**has** / **has no**) meaning.

C ▶ **5.6** Watch and study the language in the chart.

Talking about place and position	
There's a horn on the unicorn's head. Some shields are in the shape of a square.	There's a unicorn on the left / on the right. There's a lion to the left of / to the right of the shield.
There's a banner at the top. The family name is at the bottom.	The motto is above the crest. The family name is below the shield.
The shield is in front of the mantle. The mantle is behind the shield. There's a border around the shield.	Three gray flowers are in / inside the blue square. The shield is in the center / in the middle.

For more information on **prepositions of place**, see Grammar Extension 5 on page 156.

D Look at the coat of arms on page 58. Complete the sentences.

    1 The motto is _____*on*_____ the banner.

    2 The banner and motto are _____ the shield.

    3 There is a lion to the _____ of the shield.

    4 There are symbols and stripes _____ the shield.

    5 _____ the shield is a thick border.

    6 The crest is _____ the banner.

E Find and correct the mistake in each description.

    1 A "No Parking" sign in the United States is a black *P* on a white circle. There is a red border across the circle with a slash through the *P*.

    2 A stop sign in Brazil is at the shape of an octagon. It is red and has the word *Pare* (Portuguese for *stop*) written on it.

    3 A "Kangaroo Crossing" sign in Australia is a yellow diamond-shaped sign with a black image of a kangaroo below it.

F ▶ **5.7** Complete the information. Circle the correct words. Listen and check your answers.

Most countries in Europe use similar road signs. This makes it easy for visitors to understand them. For example, a yield sign is [1](**in** / **on**) the shape of an inverted triangle. It's white or yellow and has a red border [2](**across** / **around**) it. A traffic light sign is similar, but the triangle is not inverted—the wide part is at the [3](**middle** / **bottom**). There are three circles [4](**inside** / **outside**) the triangle. The one [5](**at** / **in**) the top is red. The one [6](**in** / **of**) the middle is yellow, and the bottom one is green, just like a traffic light. There are no words [7](**on** / **at**) the sign.

A traffic light sign

SPEAKING Designing a coat of arms

A You are going to design your own personal coat of arms. Look back at the coat of arms on page 58. Decide on a motto and the different design elements. Draw your design, but don't show it to anyone.

B Work in a group. Describe your coat of arms. Your group members will try to draw it.

> There are two supporters. The one on the left is a dolphin. The one on the right is a whale.

> Okay. What pattern is on the shield?

C Show your coat of arms to your group. Whose drawing is the closest to your original?

The Chicago flag can be seen all around the city.

5C Symbol of a city

PRE-READING Previewing

Look at the photo and read the third paragraph of the passage. What do the three parts of Chicago's flag represent?

1 the white areas: _____ **2** the stripes: _____ **3** the stars: _____

▶ **5.8**

1   Many cities in the United States have flags, but few are as loved as Chicago's. It can be seen all over the city—from its street corners to its skyscrapers. "Today," says Whet Moser from *Chicago* magazine, "I went to get a haircut. When I sat down in the barber's chair, there was a Chicago flag on the box that the barber kept all his **tools** in. In the mirror, there was a Chicago flag on the wall behind me. When I left, a guy passed me who had a Chicago flag on his backpack." There is even a website called ChicagoFlagTattoos.com. It features interviews with and photos of people who love the flag so much that they want it permanently drawn on their bodies.

2   The flag is also a **distinct** symbol of Chicago pride. As flag expert Ted Kaye says, "When a police officer or a firefighter dies in Chicago, often it's not the flag of the United States on his casket.[1] It can be the flag of the city of Chicago. That's how deeply the flag has gotten into the civic[2] imagery of Chicago."

3   Like any good flag, the Chicago flag's design is simple and its **symbolism** is clear. The white areas represent three Chicago neighborhoods. The stripes represent the river and the lake. The stars represent important events in Chicago's history. Its simple but **bold** design is rated highly by flag experts and is probably also the reason it has become so **popular**.

4   Roman Mars moved to Chicago in 2005, and he too fell in love with the flag. Mars is the host and creator of *99% Invisible*—a popular radio show about design and architecture. He's sure that the love for the flag is not just because people love Chicago. In Mars's own words, "I also think that people love Chicago more because the flag is so cool."

[1] **casket:** *n.* a box in which a dead person is buried

[2] **civic:** *adj.* related to a particular community

UNDERSTANDING MAIN IDEAS

Read the passage. Circle the main idea.

a The flag of Chicago is important to the identity of the city and its people.

b The flag of Chicago is a best-selling souvenir for tourists.

c The flag of Chicago became famous after being featured on a radio show.

UNDERSTANDING SUPPORTING QUOTES

Match each person to the statement that supports their quote.

1 Whet Moser ○   ○ The Chicago flag is a symbol of pride for people in the city.

2 Ted Kaye ○   ○ People like Chicago more because it has a great flag.

3 Roman Mars ○   ○ You can see the Chicago flag all around the city.

UNDERSTANDING DETAILS

Circle **T** for True, **F** for False, or **NG** for Not Given.

1 Chicago is one of few cities in the United States that has a flag. **T** **F** **NG**

2 Whet Moser has a Chicago flag tattoo. **T** **F** **NG**

3 The Chicago flag can be seen during some people's funerals. **T** **F** **NG**

4 Experts in flag design like the Chicago flag. **T** **F** **NG**

5 Roman Mars has lived in Chicago all his life. **T** **F** **NG**

BUILDING VOCABULARY

A Circle the correct option to complete each sentence.

1 **Symbolism** refers to what something _____ .

  a looks like   **b** means or represents

2 A flag with a **bold** design is _____ to see or notice.

  a easy   **b** difficult

3 If something is **popular**, many people _____ it.

  a like   **b** trust

4 An example of a barber's **tool** is _____ .

  a a customer   **b** a pair of scissors

5 A design that is **distinct** is _____ others.

  a similar to   **b** different from

B **CRITICAL THINKING**

Applying What events in your city's history could be represented on a flag? Discuss with a partner.

5D The worst-designed thing you've never noticed

TEDTALKS

ROMAN MARS tells stories about design on the radio. His **mission** is to get people to **engage with** designs they find compelling so that they begin to **pay attention to** all forms of design. He especially loves flags. His idea worth spreading is that a well-designed city flag can be an object of beauty, strengthen civic pride, and have economic benefits.

PREVIEWING

A Read the paragraph above. Circle the correct option for each sentence below. You will hear these words in the TED Talk.

1 A **mission** is something you (**need** / **don't need**) to do.

2 If you **engage with** something, you (**ignore** / **show interest in**) it.

3 When you **pay attention to** something, you (**buy** / **concentrate on**) it.

B Look at these flags of Canada and San Francisco. What do you like about each design?

VIEWING

A ▶ **5.9** Watch Part 1 of the TED Talk. Which flag does Mars prefer? Why? Discuss with a partner.

B Read the following excerpt from Part 1 of the TED Talk. How does the San Francisco flag compare with what you learned about the Chicago flag on page 60? Discuss with a partner.

"So when I moved back to San Francisco in 2008, I researched its flag, because I had never seen it in the previous eight years I lived there."

C **5.10** Complete the notes below with words from the box. Watch Part 2 of the TED Talk to check your guesses.

bigger	colors	name	enlarge
middle	simple	simplify	writing

Five principles of flag design	To improve San Francisco's flag:
1 *Keep it _____ .*	*Remove the motto.*
2 *Use meaningful symbolism.*	*Remove _____ .*
3 *Use only two to three basic _____ .*	*_____ border.*
4 *Do not use _____ of any kind.*	*Make the phoenix (bird) _____ and move to _____ .*
5 *Be distinctive.*	*_____ or stylize the phoenix.*

D ▶ **5.11** Watch Part 3 of the TED Talk. Check [✓] the statements that Mars would probably agree with.

☐ City flags can bring people together. ☐ Pocatello has a terrible flag. ☐ A good flag should have a trademark symbol.

E **CRITICAL THINKING**

Applying To design a great flag, Mars says you should first draw a rectangle of this size so that you can see it from a distance. Draw a flag you know in the space to the right. Based on this, does your flag have a good design?

VOCABULARY IN CONTEXT

▶ **5.12** Watch the excerpts from the TED Talk. Choose the correct meaning of the words.

PRESENTATION SKILLS Numbering key points

> Numbering your points in your talk (*one, two, three,* or *first, second, third,* etc.) can help your audience follow along more easily.

A ▶ **5.13** Watch the excerpt. Notice how the points are numbered.

B ▶ **5.14** Now watch excerpts of TED speaker A. J. Jacobs giving four reasons why a world family tree is important. Circle the numbers you hear.

1 One / First 2 Two / Second 3 Three / Third 4 Four / Fourth

C Work in a group. Think of three things you learned in this unit. Then share them using numbers.

> I learned three things about flags. First, most cities have them. Second, ...

5E Meaningful design

COMMUNICATE A new city flag

A Work in a group. Look at these city flags. Which one do you like the most? Which one do you like the least? Why?

B Work with a partner. You are going to design a new flag for your city. First, write down four or five things that your city is famous for. Think about famous places and historical events.

C Work together to design and sketch your flag. Keep Roman Mars's principles of design in mind.

1 Keep it simple.

2 Use meaningful symbolism.

3 Use only two to three basic colors.

4 Do not use writing of any kind.

5 Be distinctive.

D Draw your flag on a bigger sheet of paper. Then present your flag to the class. Explain what the different parts of your flag represent and any other design choices you made.

Talking about meaning
What is the meaning of …?   *It means …*
What does … represent?   *It represents …*
What does … symbolize?   *It symbolizes …*

WRITING My country's flag

Look back at the sketch you drew of the flag on page 63. Do some research and then write about what the flag means.

The design of my country's flag is very simple. It uses three colors—green, black, and white. There are three vertical stripes and in the upper left corner there is a …

6 Inspiration

" The doorbell rang and it was a trick-or-treater dressed as my character. It was so cool. "

Jarrett Krosoczka
Author, TED speaker

UNIT GOALS

In this unit, you will …

- talk about inspirational people.
- read about how someone became an author.
- watch a TED Talk about the events that inspired an author's career.

WARM UP

▶ **6.1** Watch part of Jarrett Krosoczka's TED Talk. Answer the questions with a partner.

1 What kind of books does Krosoczka write?

2 Why did Krosoczka think the trick-or-treater was "so cool"?

A boy and his father launch a model rocket.

6A Inspiring people

VOCABULARY Sources of inspiration

A ▶ 6.2 Complete the sentences with words from the box. Listen and check your answers.

changed	encouraged	gave
showed	supported	was

1 "When I met my best friend Maria, she completely _____ my life."

2 "My biology teacher, Mrs. Chang, _____ me to become a scientist."

3 "My first boss _____ a great role-model for me when I first started work."

4 "My mother _____ me that it's possible to stay positive even in difficult times."

5 "I was lucky that my parents always _____ my career in music."

6 "My grandfather always _____ me great advice when I was young."

B Change two or three of the sentences in **A** to make them true for you.

C Work with a partner. Read your sentences to each other. Ask questions as you listen.

My older brother was a great role-model for me when I was a child.

Yeah? In what way?

LISTENING My inspiration

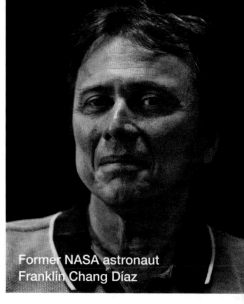

Former NASA astronaut Franklin Chang Díaz

> **Hedging**
> It is common for English speakers to use certain words or phrases to indicate uncertainty. Common hedging words include:
> *probably*   *possibly*   *maybe*   *perhaps*

A ▶ **6.3** Franklin Chang Díaz is a former NASA astronaut. Who does he describe as his "number one hero"? Watch and circle the correct answer.

    a his science teacher   **b** a famous astronaut   **c** his father

B ▶ **6.3** Watch again. Circle **T** for True or **F** for False.

   1 As an astronaut, Chang Díaz went into space only once.   **T**   **F**

   2 Chang Díaz became interested in space when he was a child.   **T**   **F**

   3 Chang Díaz's father was a scientist.   **T**   **F**

   4 Chang Díaz believes he is an inspiration for others.   **T**   **F**

C CRITICAL THINKING

Inferring Chang Díaz says that "Inspiration is in many ways a bit of a chain." What does he mean by this? Discuss with a partner.

SPEAKING Talking about an inspirational person

A ▶ **6.4** What was the music teacher's advice?

   A: When did you graduate from university?

   B: About three years ago. I kind of miss being a student.   A couple of / Just a few

   A: I know what you mean. What did you study?   did you major in / was your major

   B: Business administration. What about you?

   A: I majored in music.

   B: Yeah? Why did you choose that?

   A: I had a great music teacher at school.
      She really inspired me.   was really inspiring / was an inspiration

   B: That's cool.

   A: Yeah. She always told me to follow my passion in life.   advised me to / said that I should
      It was really great advice.

B Practice the conversation with a partner. Practice again using the words on the right.

C Think of three inspiring people. Use these examples or think of others. Tell your partner why they inspire you.

> a family member   a teacher   a leader   an athlete   a historical figure

      Serena Williams is really inspiring. She's an amazing athlete who never gives up and always wants to improve.

6B Inspiring words

LANGUAGE FOCUS Discussing inspirational people

A ▶ **6.5** Read the information. What else do you know about these people?

THE WORLD'S MOST INSPIRATIONAL PEOPLE

A recent survey identified 50 of the world's most inspiring people. Here are the top 3.

1918–2013
Former President of South Africa

NELSON MANDELA

1869–1948
Leader of independence movement in India

MAHATMA GANDHI

1955–2011
Cofounder, chairman, and CEO of Apple, Inc.

STEVE JOBS

" Education is the most powerful weapon which you can use to change the world. "

" You must be the change you wish to see in the world. "

" Innovation distinguishes between a leader and a follower. "

THESE PEOPLE ALSO MADE THE LIST: Leonardo da Vinci (Italy), Anne Frank (Germany), Frida Kahlo (Mexico), Bob Marley (Jamaica), Coco Chanel (France), Stephen Hawking (England), Martin Luther King Jr. (U.S.).

B ▶ **6.6** Listen to someone talking about two people he admires. Complete the chart.

Who does he admire?	Why does he admire them?
1	
2	

C ▶ **6.7** Watch and study the language in the chart.

Reporting what someone said		
"I admire Frida Kahlo."	He said He told me	(that) he admired Frida Kahlo.
"I don't know much about her."	He said He told me	(that) he didn't know much about her.
"Follow your dreams." "Don't be afraid."	He told me to follow my dreams. He told me not to be afraid.	

For more information on **reported speech**, see Grammar Summary 6 on page 156.

D Circle the correct option to complete each sentence.

1 My teacher (**said**/**told**) me not to interrupt while other people are talking.

2 My father (**said**/**told**) that he had two jobs when he was a student.

3 Her older brother (**said**/**told**) her to take her piano lessons more seriously.

4 My coach (**said**/**told**) me that I was his most promising new player.

5 Our professor always (**said**/**told**) us that there was no success without failure.

E Rewrite the sentences as reported speech.

1 "Think carefully about your future."   My dad told me _____ .

2 "I want to lead our country someday."   My sister said _____ .

3 "Don't make the same mistake twice."   The teacher told her _____ .

4 "I don't want to stand in your way."   My mother told me _____ .

5 "I don't worry about the little things."   My grandfather said _____ .

F ▶ **6.8** Find and correct the four mistakes in this paragraph. Listen and check your answers.

At 18 years of age, Frida Kahlo was involved in an accident that changed her life forever. Her school bus hit a streetcar, and she broke her back. She had to spend many months in bed. During this time, she discovered her love of painting. Kahlo painted many self-portraits. She once told that she painted herself because she was the subject she knew best. After her long recovery, she met painter Diego Rivera. He recognized her talent and said her to keep painting. A few years later, Rivera said that he want to marry her. She told him that she is happy to become his wife and accepted his marriage proposal. It would be the beginning of a long but difficult marriage.

Frida Kahlo

SPEAKING Getting advice

A Think of two people who gave you advice. Complete the chart with notes.

	Person	Advice
1		
2		

B Work in a group. Share your advice. Can others guess who gave you the advice (and if you took it)?

Someone told me to take up acting in high school.

Was it a teacher?

Jarrett Krosoczka offers to sign a book for a young fan.

6C Inspiring lives

PRE-READING Scanning

A Work with a partner. Look at the book cover on the right. What do you think it's about?

B Scan the text to check your idea. Do you think you'd enjoy reading the book?

▶ 6.9

1   On Jarrett Krosoczka's 14th birthday, his grandparents gave him a gift—a drawing table. During dinner that night, the fortune[1] in his fortune cookie said, "You will be successful in your work." He taped it to the table.

2   Krosoczka came from a troubled family—his parents were never around, and he had few friends. His best friends at the time were the Teenage Mutant Ninja Turtles, and other characters he read about in books. When he was in the third grade, his grandparents adopted him. "They loved me so much," he says, "and they supported my creative efforts."

3   Even as a young boy, Krosoczka loved drawing and writing stories. He was lucky in that he found **encouragement** both at home and at school. One teacher in particular stood out for him: his first-grade teacher, Mrs. Alisch. "I can just remember the love that she offered us as her students," he recalls.

4   When he was 17, he volunteered at a camp for sick children called Hole in the Wall. There he met Eric, a kid with leukemia. Eric sadly didn't live to see his sixth birthday. It was an inspirational experience that Krosoczka said changed his life—it was the pivotal[2] moment that made him want to write picture books for children.

5   After graduating from art school, Krosoczka struggled to publish his work, but he never **gave up**. He eventually published his first book, *Good Night, Monkey Boy*—a story about a young, energetic boy who never wants to go to bed. His local newspaper **celebrated** the news, and he signed copies of the book at a local bookstore. Many of the people who inspired him were present at the event, including his friends, grandparents, and even several of his teachers. Mrs. Alisch, his first-grade teacher, cut in front of the line and proudly said, "I taught him how to read." It was a very special moment for Krosoczka.

6   Krosoczka is now a successful artist. His readers clearly love his books, and he receives **fan mail** from kids all over the world. Interestingly, he still draws on that same table he got on his 14th birthday, and the fortune is still taped to it.

---

[1] **fortune:** *n.* a prediction about your future

[2] **pivotal:** *adj.* of vital or critical importance to something

UNDERSTANDING MAIN IDEAS

Choose the best subhead for each paragraph.

1 Paragraph 3	**a** Early love of art	**b** A make-believe world
2 Paragraph 4	**a** Celebrating success	**b** A writer is born
3 Paragraph 5	**a** Success at last	**b** Funny fan mail

UNDERSTANDING SEQUENCE

Number the events from 1 to 5 in the order they happened.

_____ Krosoczka published his first book.

_____ Krosoczka began to volunteer with sick children.

_____ Krosoczka graduated from art school.

_____ Krosoczka's first-grade teacher attended his book signing.

_____ Krosoczka got a fortune cookie that said he would be successful.

UNDERSTANDING DETAILS

Match the two parts of the sentences.

1 The Teenage Mutant Ninja Turtles ○	○ adopted him.
2 Krosoczka's grandparents ○	○ taught him to read.
3 Krosoczka's parents ○	○ sent him fan mail.
4 Eric ○	○ inspired him to write children's books.
5 Mrs. Alisch ○	○ were never around.
6 Kids around the world ○	○ were his best friends.

BUILDING VOCABULARY

A Circle the correct option to complete each sentence.

1 You give **encouragement** when you want someone to _____ .

   a keep trying   **b** stop what they're doing

2 If you **gave up** during a competition, you _____ .

   a quit   **b** won

3 Students are likely to **celebrate** when they _____ an exam.

   a pass   **b** fail

4 You might send **fan mail** to _____ .

   a a family member   **b** a famous person you like

B **CRITICAL THINKING**

Evaluating What do you think are the best things about being a children's author? What are the challenges? Discuss with a partner.

6D How a boy became an artist

TEDTALKS

JARRETT KROSOCZKA is an author and **illustrator**. In his TED Talk he describes a **compliment** he received that made a **colossal** difference in his life. His idea worth spreading is that inspiration often comes to us in unexpected ways and that we can use our own talents to inspire others.

PREVIEWING

Read the paragraph above. Circle the correct option for each sentence below. You will hear these words in the TED Talk.

1 The **illustrator** of a book is the person who (**writes it** / **draws the pictures**).

2 If you give a **compliment,** you say something (**nice** / **bad**) about someone.

3 A **colossal** failure is a (**very big** / **really small**) failure.

VIEWING

A ▶ **6.10** Watch Part 1 of the TED Talk. Circle the correct answers.

1 Who was Jack Gantos?

   a an author   **b** a teacher

2 How did Gantos inspire Krosoczka?

   a He complimented Krosoczka on his drawing.   **b** He helped Krosoczka write a story.

3 What did Krosoczka start to do after school?

   a write letters to famous authors   **b** write his own stories

B ▶ **6.11** Watch Part 2 of the TED Talk. Check [✓] each box to show if the statement refers to Mr. Greenwood or Mr. Lynch. Some statements refer to both.

	Mr. Greenwood	Mr. Lynch
a complimented him on his drawing	☐	☐
b said he should be the school cartoonist	☐	☐
c asked him to stop drawing in class	☐	☐
d told him to forget everything he learned	☐	☐

C ▶ **6.12** Watch Part 3 of the TED Talk. Work with a partner. Explain why each thing below is important to Krosoczka.

   a an email that said, "Nice work!"   **b** the date June 12, 2001   **c** a Monkey Boy birthday cake

D CRITICAL THINKING

Inferring Why do you think Krosoczka has a framed photo of the Monkey Boy cake on his desk?

VOCABULARY IN CONTEXT

▶ **6.13** Watch the excerpts from the TED Talk. Choose the correct meaning of the words.

PRESENTATION SKILLS Using your voice effectively

You can make your presentation clearer and more memorable by using your voice effectively. You can raise or lower your voice, stress words, vary your speed, pause, or even change your voice to indicate you're quoting another person.

A ▶ **6.14** Watch part of Jarrett Krosoczka's TED Talk. Notice how he speaks very softly when he's telling the story of the visiting author. Why do you think he does this?

B ▶ **6.15** Now watch two other TED speakers. What does each person do with his voice? Choose the correct answers.

1 A. J. Jacobs

   a   He speeds up and stresses key words.   **b**   He slows down and speaks very softly.

2 Roman Mars

   a   He makes his voice much higher.   **b**   He slows down and pauses between words.

C Work with a partner. Read the text below in different ways. How does the meaning change?

| emphasizing key words | pausing at key moments | using your grandmother's voice |

My grandmother was an inspiration to me. One day I was upset with a grade I got at school, and she said, "Just do your best. No one should expect more than that." I looked at her for a moment but didn't say a word. And deep in my heart, I knew she was right.

6E A world of inspiration

COMMUNICATE A lively dinner party

A Work alone. Write a list of people that you find inspirational. Think about people from the following categories.

| political figures | athletes | musicians | entertainers |
| writers | artists | adventurers | scientists |

B Work with a partner. Imagine you are having a small dinner party for eight people (including you and your partner). You can invite anybody you like from your lists of inspirational people. Decide on six people to invite. Give reasons for your answers.

Asking about what someone knows
Do you know …?   Have you heard of …?   Are you familiar with …?

C Now decide on the seating plan. You want an interesting party with a lively discussion of ideas. Decide who should and shouldn't sit where.

D Work with another pair. Describe your dinner party and give reasons for your seating plan.

WRITING An inspiring person

Who do you think is inspirational? Write about them. It could be a famous person or someone you know personally. What makes the person so inspirational to you?

My older sister Rebecca has always been a great role-model for me. She's always been very ambitious and has worked so hard to get where she is today. She's shown me that anything is possible as long as you try your best.

Presentation 2

MODEL PRESENTATION

A Complete the transcript of the presentation using the words in the box.

around	bright	gave	little	much
on	relaxed	said	showed	told

Today, I want to tell you about a person who made a huge difference in my life—my first teacher, Mrs. Daniels. When I was young, I was extremely shy and had very ¹_____ self-confidence. I remember being so nervous on my first day at school. But Mrs. Daniels was so kind and friendly that I soon forgot about that. In that first class, Mrs. Daniels asked us all to draw a picture of ourselves to put ²_____ the classroom wall. She walked ³_____ the classroom patiently helping everyone. When she got to my desk, she looked at my picture and ⁴_____, "Wow! Look at those ⁵_____ colors! That's great!" I immediately felt ⁶_____. But that wasn't all. Mrs. Daniels was my teacher for one year, and she helped me become a lot more confident. She always praised us and encouraged us to express ourselves. She ⁷_____ us not to worry about giving wrong answers in class and ⁸_____ us how to learn from our mistakes. Even today, I still remember all the advice that Mrs. Daniels ⁹_____ me. I think without her, I would be a different person. I owe her so ¹⁰_____.

Thank you for listening.

B ▶ **P.2** Watch the presentation and check your answers.

C ▶ **P.2** Review the list of presentation skills from Units 1–6 below. Which does the speaker use? Check [✓] each skill used as you watch again.

The speaker …
- ☐ uses questions to signpost
- ☐ personalizes the presentation
- ☐ closes the presentation effectively
- ☐ provides background information
- ☐ numbers key points
- ☐ uses their voice effectively

YOUR TURN

A You are going to plan and give a short presentation to a partner about a great teacher you once had. Use some or all of the questions below to make some notes.

> What was the teacher's name?
>
> What did they teach?
>
> Why were they a great teacher?
>
> What advice did the teacher give you?
>
> How did the teacher affect your life?

B Look at the useful phrases in the box below. Think about which ones you will need in your presentation.

> **Useful phrases**
>
> Giving background information: *When I was ... / As a child ... / Before I ...*
>
> Describing inspiration: *changed my life / encouraged me / gave me advice / showed me / supported me / was a role-model*
>
> Reporting what someone said: *said that / told me that / advised me to*
>
> Describing effects: *I'll always remember ... / Since then, I ... I'll never forget ...*

C Work with a partner. Take turns giving your presentation using your notes. Use some of the presentation skills from Units 1–6. As you listen, check [✓] each skill your partner uses.

> The speaker ...
> - ☐ uses questions to signpost
> - ☐ personalizes the presentation
> - ☐ closes the presentation effectively
> - ☐ provides background information
> - ☐ numbers key points
> - ☐ uses their voice effectively

D Give your partner some feedback on their talk. Include two things you liked, and one thing he or she can improve.

> That was great. You used your voice really well and provided lots of background information. Next time, try to smile a bit more.

7 Ethical Choices

> **«** I'm convinced that in 30 years, when we look back on today and on how we raise and slaughter billions of animals ... we'll see this as being wasteful and indeed crazy. **»**

Andras Forgacs
Bioprinting entrepreneur, TED speaker

UNIT GOALS

In this unit, you will ...

- talk about ethical choices.
- read about a process called biofabrication.
- watch a TED Talk about a way to produce meat and leather more ethically.

WARM UP

▶ **7.1** Watch part of Andras Forgacs's TED Talk. Answer the questions with a partner.

1 What does Forgacs say we'll think in the future?

2 Why do you think he feels this way?

7A Food choices

An organic farm in
British Columbia, Canada

VOCABULARY Ethical food choices

A ▶ **7.2** Complete each definition using the words in the box. Watch and check your answers.

fair trade	free-range	organic
locally produced	genetically modified	sustainable

1 _____ food is grown naturally, without using any special chemicals.

2 On _____ farms, animals are not kept in cages and can move around.

3 _____ food is grown using technology to change the food's size, color, taste, etc.

4 _____ food production aims to provide better trading and working conditions for farmers in developing countries.

5 By choosing _____ food, you minimize the distance the food needs to travel. This helps the environment.

6 _____ food production aims to preserve the world's natural resources for the future.

B Which of the things in **A** do you consider when you buy food? Discuss with a partner. Explain your answers.

To be honest, I only really think about the quality and price.

I always consider whether the food I buy is locally produced or not. I like to support local businesses.

LISTENING Sustainable chef

Barton Seaver

> **Identifying main ideas in fast speech**
> Many native speakers talk quickly but will often slow down to emphasize key points. Focusing on these slower parts of speech can help identify the speaker's main message.

A ▶ **7.3** Barton Seaver is a chef and environmentalist. Watch. What did he once work as in Africa? Circle the correct answer.

   a a farmer   **b** a fisherman   **c** a trader

B ▶ **7.3** Watch again. Complete the sentences with the words you hear.

   1 "_____ is how the vast majority of us interact with our resources."

   2 "Environmentalism is so often thought of as this _____ idea."

   3 "But _____ is full contact environmentalism."

C **CRITICAL THINKING**

Interpreting Work with a partner. Explain in your own words what Seaver means by each quote in **B** above.

SPEAKING Talking about ethical choices

A ▶ **7.4** Why did the woman switch to organic food?

   A: I think that's all I need. How about you?

   B: Let me just get some apples, and I'll be ready.   done / finished

   A: Why don't you get these? They look nice.

   B: Oh, I only eat organic fruits and vegetables now.

   A: Really? Why?   Why's that / How come

   B: I decided I didn't want to eat food that is grown using chemicals. I heard it's not very good for you.

   A: That makes sense.   I can see that / I can understand that

   B: And it's better for the environment.

   A: But does that mean you have to pay higher prices?   pay more / spend more

   B: Not necessarily. It depends where you shop.

B Practice the conversation with a partner. Practice again using the words on the right.

C Work with a partner. Which of these things do you buy more often? Why?

free-range or regular eggs	locally produced or imported food	regular or organic fruit

7B What the future holds

LANGUAGE FOCUS Discussing the future

A ▶ **7.5** Read the information. Which two countries saw the biggest increase in meat consumption between 1961 and 2011? What do you think was the reason? Discuss with a partner.

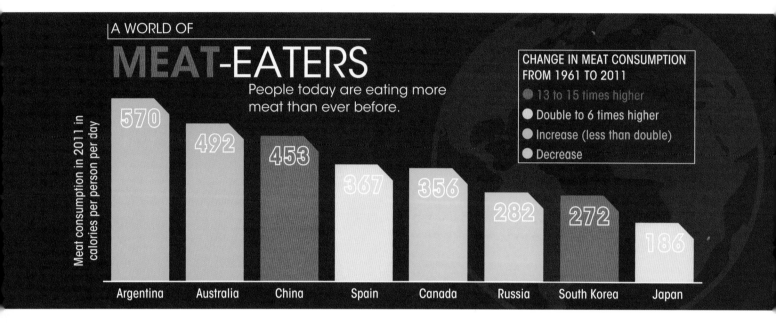

A WORLD OF

MEAT-EATERS
People today are eating more meat than ever before.

Meat consumption in 2011 in calories per person per day

570 Argentina
492 Australia
453 China
367 Spain
356 Canada
282 Russia
272 South Korea
186 Japan

CHANGE IN MEAT CONSUMPTION FROM 1961 TO 2011
- 13 to 15 times higher
- Double to 6 times higher
- Increase (less than double)
- Decrease

B ▶ **7.6** An expert is talking about the data above. Watch and complete the predictions.

1 In the future, the global demand for meat will (**probably** / **definitely**) increase.

2 By 2050, the world's population will increase by about (**15** / **35**) percent.

3 There will be a (**100** / **150**) percent increase in demand for meat from developing countries.

C ▶ **7.7** Watch and study the language in the chart.

Making predictions	
In the future, more people will eat meat. It won't be easy to meet this demand. Will it have an effect on the environment?	Yes, it will. / No, it won't.
The price of meat will definitely / probably be higher in the future. There definitely / probably won't be enough meat for everyone.	
When will the world's population reach 10 billion people?	It will reach 10 billion by around 2050 / in about 30 years.

For more information on **will for predictions**, see Grammar Summary 7 on page 157.

D ▶ **7.6** Circle the correct option to complete the sentences from the conversation. Listen again to check your answers.

1 Today, people around the world (**are eating**/**will eat**) more meat than ever before.

2 Do you think this trend (**is continuing**/**will continue**) in the future?

3 Every day, there (**are**/**will be**) 228,000 more people on the planet.

4 By 2050, many more people (**are able to**/**will be able to**) buy meat regularly.

5 In the next 30 years, there (**is**/**will be**) a huge rise in the number of people demanding meat.

E ▶ **7.8** Read the information. Find and correct the three mistakes. Listen and check your answers.

According to a recent report, climate change has started to affect farmers around the world. Although some crops will definitely grow better in a warmer world, others won't probably do so well.

The report predicts that yields of crops like corn, wheat, and rice will start to decrease in 2030. They probably decline by up to 2 percent for each decade after that.

Other crops, such as fruit and nut trees, will also be affected. Almonds need a long period of cool weather each year. Without this, trees won't flower. Other crops that will be definitely under threat in the next few decades are grapes, cherries, and apples.

Avocados hang from a dying tree in California.

SPEAKING Predicting future habits

A Look at the questions below. Complete the table with your own predictions.

Do you think _____ in the future?	Yes or no?	Reason
people in your country will eat more meat		
meat will be more expensive in your country		
you will change your eating habits		
people around the world will have enough to eat		
most people in the world will be healthier		

B Work with a partner. Take turns asking the questions above. Give reasons for your answers. Were your predictions the same?

> Do you think people in your country will eat more meat in the future?

> No, I don't. People in this country already eat a lot of meat.

Over a billion animals a year are killed to make leather products like these.

7C Leather from a lab

PRE-READING Previewing

A How many leather products do you own? Discuss with a partner.

B Read the first paragraph of the passage. What is the problem with leather?

▶ **7.9**

1   Leather is a hugely popular material for a **range** of products: shoes, jackets, bags, wallets—the list goes on. But this popularity comes at a price. The global leather industry kills
5 over a billion animals every year. This has caused many to ask the question: Is it possible to meet the global demand of leather but not do any harm to animals? A process called biofabrication may be the answer.
10   Biofabrication is not new; it is already commonly used in medicine. Biofabrication techniques are used to grow body parts like ears, skin, and bones for transplants.[1] But it can also be used to make other products, such as leather. Biofabricated
15 leather has many advantages. Scientists will be able to make it with whatever qualities they want, such as extra softness, greater strength, or even different colors and patterns.

    But how exactly does biofabrication work?
20 To grow leather, scientists begin by taking some cells from an animal, not hurting the animal in any way. They then isolate the cells and grow them in a **lab**. This process takes millions of cells and expands them into billions. Next, the scientists take
25 the cells and spread them out to form thin sheets. These thin sheets are then **layered** to combine into thicker sheets. After that, the scientists can tan the hide.[2] Anyone can then dye[3] and finish the leather and design it in any way they like—into bags,
30 watches, or shoes.

    Andras Forgacs supports biofabrication. He says it may even be a "natural evolution[4] of manufacturing for mankind." We will be able to make the products we need in a more **efficient**,
35 responsible, and creative way. And biofabrication is not just about leather—it's possible the technique could also be used to grow meat. While this may sound crazy, Forgacs certainly doesn't think so. "What's crazy," he says, "is what we do today."

[1] **transplant:** *n.* an operation in which a body part is replaced
[2] **tan the hide:** *phrase* to turn animal skin into leather
[3] **dye:** *v.* to change the color of something using special liquid
[4] **evolution:** *n.* a process of gradual, natural change over time

UNDERSTANDING DETAILS

Read the passage. Circle **T** for true, **F** for false, or **NG** for not given.

1 Many animals are killed to make leather.   T   F   NG

2 Demand for leather is increasing.   T   F   NG

3 Biofabrication is already used in medicine.   T   F   NG

4 Animals feel pain when scientists take their cells.   T   F   NG

5 Andras Forgacs is in favor of biofabrication.   T   F   NG

6 Biofabrication could be used to grow meat.   T   F   NG

UNDERSTANDING A PROCESS

Look at the diagram. Number the sentences 1–8.

_____ Scientists grow the cells in a lab.

_____ Scientists can tan the hide.

_____ Thicker sheets are formed.

_____ Scientists spread the cells and form thin sheets.

_____ Scientists take cells from an animal.

_____ The thin sheets are layered.

_____ The leather can by dyed and finished.

_____ The leather is made into different products.

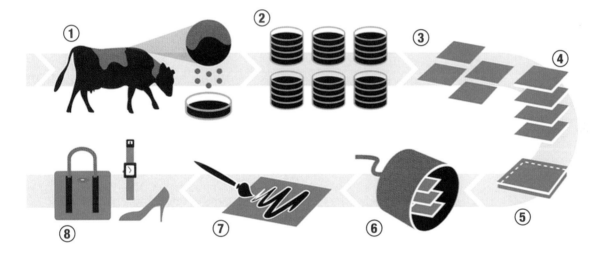

BUILDING VOCABULARY

A Match each word in **blue** from the passage to its definition.

1 range   ○   ○   a room where scientific experiments take place

2 cell   ○   ○   able to do something well without wasting time or energy

3 lab   ○   ○   an extremely small part of an animal or plant

4 layer   ○   ○   a number of different things

5 efficient   ○   ○   to arrange one on top of another

B CRITICAL THINKING

Personalizing Would you wear biofabricated leather? Would you eat biofabricated meat? Discuss with a partner.

7D Leather and meat without killing animals

TEDTALKS

When **ANDRAS FORGACS** started a company to 3D-print human **tissues** and **organs**, people thought he was crazy. But after some success, he realized he could also grow products like meat and leather to avoid the **slaughter** of animals. Forgacs's idea worth spreading is that we can be more efficient and **humane** by getting meat and leather from tissues grown in a lab.

PREVIEWING

A Read the paragraph above. Circle the correction option for each sentence below. You will hear these words in the TED Talk.

1 **Tissues** are materials that (**living things** / **machines**) are made from.

2 An example of a human **organ** is your (**brain** / **foot**).

3 When you **slaughter** an animal, you (**kill** / **save**) it.

4 A **humane** person is (**kind and gentle** / **mean and angry**).

B Look at the photo on page 85. What does Forgacs's presentation slide show?

VIEWING

A ▶ **7.10** Watch Part 1 of the TED Talk. Check [✓] the reasons why Forgacs is concerned about having a herd of 100 billion farm animals on the planet.

☐ The animals will use large amounts of land and water.

☐ The animals will produce even more greenhouse gases.

☐ It will cause many wild animals to become extinct.

☐ Diseases will spread more easily.

B ▶ **7.11** Watch Part 2 of the TED Talk. Why does Forgacs think producing leather is a good place for biofabrication to begin? Check [✓] each reason he mentions.

☐ It's widely used. ☐ It's cheap. ☐ It's simple to grow.

☐ It's beautiful. ☐ It's part of our history. ☐ It's strong.

C ▶ **7.12** Watch Part 3 of the TED Talk. Complete Forgacs's description of biofabricated leather. Match the two parts of each sentence.

Benefits of biofabricated leather

1 It is just like regular leather because it is made from ○ ○ a cow or alligator.

2 It doesn't have ○ ○ its properties.

3 It can be grown in the shape of ○ ○ the same cells.

4 It is not limited to the shape of ○ ○ a wallet or handbag.

5 We can control ○ ○ hair, scars, or insect bites.

D CRITICAL THINKING

Applying Which of these groups do you think would support biofabrication? Why? Discuss with a partner.

vegetarians	farmers	animal ranchers	fashion designers

VOCABULARY IN CONTEXT

▶ **7.13** Watch the excerpts from the TED Talk. Choose the correct meaning of the words.

PRESENTATION SKILLS Creating effective slides

It pays to take the time to make your presentation slides as effective as possible. The following tips can help you.

Keep the background plain.   *Use strong, contrasting colors.*
Do not use too much text.   *Keep any graphics or images simple.*

A ▶ **7.14** Watch part of Andras Forgacs's TED Talk. Notice how effective his slide is.

B ▶ **7.15** Now watch Forgacs show another slide. Do you think it's effective? Why or why not? Use the tips in the box above to help you decide.

7E Looking ahead

COMMUNICATE Weighing both sides

A Work in a group. The year is 2050. A company wants to open a biofabrication factory in your city. The factory will produce biofabricated meat and leather. Brainstorm some arguments for and against opening the factory. Write notes in the box below. Consider the following:

the effect on jobs	the effect on animals	people's health
the quality of food	the environment	the price of food

Arguments for the biofabrication lab	Arguments against the biofabrication lab

B Split into two groups. **Group A** is in favor of the biofabrication factory. **Group B** is against it. You are going to give a presentation to argue your position. Choose three or four of the strongest arguments. Prepare some slides to help get your points across.

C Present your arguments and your slides to another group. Take notes as you listen.

> **Acknowledging a point**
> *That's a good point, but … I see what you mean, but … I can see your point, but …*

WRITING The future of food

Are you more optimistic or pessimistic about the future of food? Support your idea with at least three predictions of what you think the future will be like.

> I am optimistic about the future of food. I think scientists will continue to find new, creative ways to feed our population. They will also find ways to make food more nutritious.

8 Better Cities

"Things that you and I might think about as global problems, like climate change, the energy crisis or poverty, are really, in many ways, city problems."

Alessandra Orofino
Political mobilization activist, TED speaker

UNIT GOALS

In this unit, you will …

- talk about what makes a great city.
- read about possible solutions to city problems.
- watch a TED Talk about how technology can help solve urban problems.

WARM UP

▶ **8.1** Watch part of Alessandra Orofino's TED Talk. Answer the questions with a partner.

1 What examples of city problems does Orofino give?

2 What are some positive aspects of cities?

Vancouver, Canada

8A What makes a great city?

VOCABULARY Features of a city

A Complete the chart below using the words in the box.

| galleries | industrial park | lively |
| multicultural | museums | suburbs |

Areas of a city	Things to enjoy	Words to describe a city
residential area riverfront	theaters markets	bustling modern

B Work with a partner. Add one more word to each column.

C Work with a partner. What are the best things about your town or city? Why?

> I really like the riverfront area. It's a great place to hang out.

> I agree. I like the cafés and restaurants there.

LISTENING Living abroad

A ▶ **8.2** Claire Street is talking about three different countries she has lived
in. Watch and write the names of the countries.

1 She grew up in a town called Whitworth in _____ .

2 She moved to _____ when she was 21.

3 Now she lives in _____ .

B ▶ **8.2** Watch again. How does Street describe the three different
places she's lived in? Which place do you think is her favorite?

C **CRITICAL THINKING**

Analyzing Would you like to live in any of the places Street talks
about? Why or why not? Discuss with a partner.

Claire Street

SPEAKING Talking about where you live

A ▶ **8.3** What do the two people like about living in Brisbane?

A: How do you like living in Brisbane so far?

B: Oh, I love it. It's such a busy place. You grew up here,   multicultural / lively
didn't you?

A: Actually, I was born in a small town near here called
Toowoomba, but I moved here about seven years ago.

B: What's your favorite part of the city?   area / place

A: Well, I really like the South Bank Parklands.
I know a few nice restaurants there.   cafés / shops

B: Yeah?

A: Yeah, it's a great place to hang out with friends.   meet up / spend time

B: Cool. I should check it out sometime.

B Practice the conversation with a partner. Practice again using the words on the right.

C Work with a partner. What city would you like to live in someday? Why?

> I'd love to live in Madrid someday. I'd like to learn Spanish.

> But why Madrid and not another Spanish city?

8B Happy cities

LANGUAGE FOCUS Talking about cities

A ▶ 8.4 Read the information. Which of these cities would you like to live in?

THE BEST CITIES IN THE WORLD

These four cities rank among the top ten happiest in the world. What makes each city's residents so happy?

MONTERREY, MEXICO
- a high standard of living
- a bustling city center
- an excellent transportation system

AARHUS, DENMARK
- closeness to nature
- variety of restaurants
- sense of community

DUBAI, UNITED ARAB EMIRATES
- a high standard of living
- an excellent transportation system
- world-class shopping

AUCKLAND, NEW ZEALAND
- excellent restaurants
- a bustling city center
- a multicultural population

B ▶ 8.5 Listen to two people talking about one of the places above. Complete the sentences.

1 The man grew up in (**Aarhus** / **Monterrey**).

2 He liked hanging out with his friends at the (**beach** / **riverfront**).

3 He used to get around by (**bus** / **car**).

C ▶ 8.6 Watch and study the language in the chart.

Using phrasal verbs	
Not separable	
I grew up in this neighborhood.	The mall is a good place to hang out with friends.
The bus is the best way to get around.	I meet up with my friends every weekend.
What do you look for in a city?	I'm looking forward to visiting Dubai.
Separable	
They need to clean up their city.	~~They need to clean up it.~~
They need to clean their city up.	They need to clean it up.
Let's check out some new plays.	~~Let's check out them.~~
Let's check some new plays out.	Let's check them out.

For more information on **phrasal verbs**, see Grammar Summary 8 on page 157.

D Find and correct three mistakes in the conversation below.

A: I can't wait for the weekend.

B: Yeah. I'm really looking forward it to.

A: Do you want to check out the new *Star Wars* movie?

B: Good idea. We can meet up with Dave, too.

A: Yeah. It's been a while since I hung out him.

B: OK. I'll probably drive, so I can pick up you.

E Complete these questions using a phrasal verb from the box. Use a dictionary if necessary. Then ask and answer the questions with a partner.

get around	grow up	hang out with	look for

1 Where did you _____?

2 Is it easy to _____ by public transportation in your city?

3 What's a fun place to _____ your friends?

4 What do you _____ in a place to live?

F ▶ **8.7** Circle the correct words. Use a dictionary to help you. Listen and check your answers.

San Sebastián, Spain, must be one of the most beautiful cities in the world. It's a fantastic place to live, but it's also a great place for tourists to visit.

Kick ¹(**through**/**back**/**apart**) at one of its four main beaches, eat ²(**off**/**out**/**by**) at one of its many restaurants, or head ³(**up**/**for**/**against**) the amusement park to get the best view of the city. Whatever you end ⁴(**up**/**in**/**off**) doing, you will have a memorable time.

There are always cultural events going ⁵(**on**/**in**/**at**) in the city. Check ⁶(**down**/**out**/**up**) a museum, take ⁷(**off**/**of**/**in**) some live theater, or spend some time at one of its many festivals. In fact, the city was named a European Capital of Culture in 2016.

San Sebastián, Spain

SPEAKING Talking about best places

A Work with a partner. Discuss the questions and note your answers.

Where's the best place in your city to …?

eat out on a budget _____

spend a rainy afternoon _____

get around by bicycle _____

chill out and do nothing _____

B Join another pair and compare your ideas.

Rio de Janeiro, Brazil

8C Connecting citizens

PRE-READING Discussion

A Do you think people who live in cities are happier than other people? Discuss with a partner.

B Read the passage. What does Alessandra Orofino think?

▶ 8.8

1   Urban activist Alessandra Orofino's home city of Rio de Janeiro is one of the world's megacities. With a population of over 11 million, Rio has grown extremely quickly over the last 60 years. But Rio is not unique. Cities around the world are growing at similar speeds. Today, around half the world's population lives in cities, and nearly 2 billion new residents are expected in the next 20 years.

2   Cities are growing because of the advantages they offer. Residents are provided with convenience,[1] culture, and jobs. But Orofino believes that modern city life is far from ideal.

3   According to Orofino, people are becoming increasingly disconnected with the cities they live in. **Election** turnouts[2] in cities around the world are falling. In Rio, for example, voting is **required** by law. However, in one election, nearly 30 percent of people did not **vote**; instead they stayed home and chose to **pay a fine** instead.

4   Orofino also believes that cities cause us to be disconnected from one another. As new buildings are built, many public spaces disappear. Without these places, it's difficult for people to socialize,[3] make friends, and form a close and happy community.

5   Orofino believes that getting **citizens** to work together and be more involved with the running of their cities is hugely important. To this end, Orofino cofounded[4] a group called Meu Rio. Meu Rio is an online network that makes it easier for Rio citizens to have their say about the running of the city. As part of the network, people receive news updates and are able to participate in important decisions about the future of their city.

6   Meu Rio has been a huge success. More than 200,000 Rio citizens are now part of this online community. Orofino is hopeful that projects like hers will become common in cities around the world, and will start what she calls "a participation revolution."

[1] **convenience:** *n.* a situation where things are easy to do
[2] **turnout:** *n.* the number of people who go to an event

[3] **socialize:** *v.* to meet and talk to different people
[4] **cofound:** *v.* to start an organization together with another person

UNDERSTANDING PURPOSE

What's the main purpose of the passage? Circle the correct answer.

a to explain the benefits of living in cities

b to highlight problems of cities and offer a possible solution

c to show what Rio de Janeiro learned from other cities

UNDERSTANDING MAIN IDEAS

Match each paragraph with its main idea.

Paragraph 1   ○   ○   Residents are becoming disconnected from their cities.

Paragraph 2   ○   ○   As cities grow, there are fewer close communities.

Paragraph 3   ○   ○   Cities around the world are growing.

Paragraph 4   ○   ○   Cities have their good points but they also have problems.

Paragraph 5   ○   ○   Orofino hopes other cities will start a project like hers.

Paragraph 6   ○   ○   Orofino started an organization to help involve Rio citizens in the running of their city.

UNDERSTANDING DETAILS

Circle **T** for true, **F** for false, or **NG** for not given.

1 Rio de Janeiro is the fastest-growing city in Brazil.	**T**	**F**	**NG**
2 The number of people living in cities around the world is rising.	**T**	**F**	**NG**
3 In cities around the world, election turnouts are increasing.	**T**	**F**	**NG**
4 People in Rio de Janeiro are required to vote by law.	**T**	**F**	**NG**
5 Orofino started Meu Rio in 2011.	**T**	**F**	**NG**
6 Members of Meu Rio receive news updates via the Internet.	**T**	**F**	**NG**
7 Meu Rio has more than 200,000 members.	**T**	**F**	**NG**

BUILDING VOCABULARY

A Complete the paragraph with the words in **blue** from the passage.

When a country holds a(n) ¹_____, it's an opportunity for
²_____ to ³_____ or to make their voices heard
on relevant issues. In about two dozen countries, including Argentina, Greece,
and Australia, people are ⁴_____ to participate in the process. If
they choose not to, they have to ⁵_____ or perform community
service.

B CRITICAL THINKING

Personalizing **Does your town or city have similar problems to those described in the article? Discuss with a partner.**

It's our city. Let's fix it.

TEDTALKS

In spite of their problems, **ALESSANDRA OROFINO** calls cities "the greatest **invention** of our time." She works with an organization that empowers Rio de Janeiro citizens to start **campaigns** to initiate change in their city. Her idea worth spreading is that we can use technology to harness "people power" and fix big problems in the world's cities.

PREVIEWING

Read the paragraph above. Match each **bold** word to its meaning. You will hear these words in the TED Talk.

1 something that has been newly created: _____

2 even with: _____

3 activities designed to show a result: _____

VIEWING

A ▶ **8.9** Watch Part 1 of the TED Talk. Match the information to complete the statistics Orofino gives.

1 The percentage of the world's population that lives in cities.	○	○	80%
2 The percentage of global energy consumption that occurs in cities.	○	○	75%
3 The percentage of global gas emissions that come from cities.	○	○	54%
4 The percentage of Meu Rio members who are aged 20–29.	○	○	40%

B ▶ **8.10** Watch Part 2 of the TED Talk. Orofino describes three members of her organization. Complete the notes.

Bia	Jovita	Leandro
• _____-year-old girl • government wanted to demolish her _____ to build a parking lot • used Meu Rio to start a campaign • the government changed their minds	• her _____ went missing around _____ years ago • found out Rio had no system to find missing persons • used Meu Rio to start a campaign to create a system • secretary of security received _____ emails • a police unit was set up	• lives in a slum • created a _____ project • received an order from the government saying he had to _____ the area in 2 weeks • used Meu Rio to start a campaign • the government changed their minds

C ▶ **8.11** Watch Part 3 of the TED Talk. Choose the correct option to complete each sentence.

1 Orofino says the stories make her happy because _____.

   a the lives of the people have changed   **b** she knew the people personally

2 Next, Orofino wants to _____.

   a share what she has learned   **b** develop the Meu Rio technology even further

D **CRITICAL THINKING**

Analyzing Could the "people power" solutions that Orofino discusses work in your city? If not, why?

VOCABULARY IN CONTEXT

▶ **8.12** Watch the excerpts from the TED Talk. Choose the correct meaning of the words.

PRESENTATION SKILLS Using anecdotes

> A speaker may choose to use an anecdote to make a point. Anecdotes can be powerful tools. An audience often reacts emotionally to a true story.

A ▶ **8.13** Watch part of Orofino's talk. Notice how effective her anecdote is.

B ▶ **8.14** These TED speakers used anecdotes to make a point. Do you remember what they were? Match each speaker to the correct anecdote. Watch the excerpts to check your answers.

1 Ann Morgan   o   o   a time when someone famous visited their school

2 Daria van den Bercken   o   o   a time when they discovered something on the Internet

3 Jarrett Krosoczka   o   o   a time when they learned something about themselves

C Work in a group. Imagine you are going to give a presentation. Choose one of these topics. Prepare and tell a short anecdote.

inspiration	kindness	friendship	honesty	change

I once ordered a coffee, but when I went to pay, I realized I didn't have my purse. The woman behind me in line offered to buy the coffee for me. It was so kind!

Rio de Janeiro's downtown skyline

COMMUNICATE Let's fix this!

A Your city has a problem with lost pets. When a pet gets lost, there is no way to track or find it. The local government wants someone to design a smartphone app to help. Work in a group. Brainstorm ways an app could help solve the problem.

> An app could help you track your pet's location.

> Good idea! How would that work?

B Choose the best ideas and work together to design your app. Complete the notes below.

> Name of app:
>
> What can it do?
>
> How does it work?

> **Giving examples**
>
> *For example, ...*   *For instance, ...*   *such as ...*

C Work with another group. Compare your ideas. Which app do you think would be best at solving the problem?

WRITING A change for the better

Imagine you are allowed to make one change—big or small—to your city. What would you do? Why?

> One problem with my city is that it doesn't use enough renewable energy. Most of the city's power comes from an old gas power plant, and I don't think this is good for the environment. If I could make a change, I'd like to ...

A dog is fitted with an electronic tracking device.

9 Giving

John Holcroft

" ... To a veteran aid worker, the idea of putting cold, hard cash into the hands of the poorest people on Earth doesn't sound crazy, it sounds really satisfying. **"**

Joy Sun
Aid worker, TED speaker

UNIT GOALS

In this unit, you will ...

- talk about giving to charities and causes.
- read about technology that is changing how charities work.
- watch a TED Talk about a different way to donate money.

WARM UP

▶ **9.1** Watch part of Joy Sun's TED Talk. Answer the questions with a partner.

1 According to Sun, what do many aid workers want to do?

2 Why do you think they might feel this way?

A baby pink river dolphin is rescued from illegal traders, Amazon River, Peru

9A A helping hand

VOCABULARY Helping others

A Look at the phrases. ~~Cross out~~ the option that doesn't belong.

1 donate	money	time	social work
2 raise	volunteers	money	awareness
3 make	a cause	a donation	a difference
4 hold	a fundraiser	a charity	an event
5 support	a cause	a charity	money

B Work with a partner. Think of at least one charity for each category below.

Health	Environmental	Animal welfare

C Choose one or two charities from **B**. Explain what they do.

Save the Children raises awareness of children's rights.

Yeah, and they raise money for better health care and education.

LISTENING My fundraising adventure

> **Understanding directions**
> The nouns *north*, *south*, *east*, and *west* are also often used as adverbs to describe a direction of movement.
> *go north*   *head south*   *sail east*   *fly west*

A ▶ **9.2** Watch Neil Glover talking about a time he raised money for charity. What did he do to raise money?

    a He walked 100 km.   **b** He sailed across an ocean.   **c** He drove around a country.

B ▶ **9.2** Watch again. Circle **T** for true or **F** for false.

    1 The event took place in England.   **T**   **F**

    2 The journey took eight days.   **T**   **F**

    3 Glover and his friends raised money online.   **T**   **F**

    4 Glover's team raised $170,000.   **T**   **F**

C CRITICAL THINKING

    Personalizing Would you like to take part in the event Glover described? Why or why not? Discuss with a partner.

Neil Glover with local children during his fundraising journey

SPEAKING Talking about good causes

A ▶ **9.3** What are the two people talking about?

    A: Oh, my sister just texted me. She asked me to donate some money to charity.

    B: What type of charity?

    A: She's trying to raise money to help save the rain forest.   for an animal charity / for cancer research

    B: That's great!

    A: Yeah. Last year, she ran a marathon to help raise awareness. She also set up a website.   held an event / held a fundraiser

    B: So, how much do you think you'll give?   donate / contribute

    A: Hmm. I think I'll donate $20.

    B: OK. Well, if you give $20, I will, too. After all, it's for a really good cause.   worthy / worthwhile

B Practice the conversation with a partner. Practice again using the words on the right.

C Think about a time you helped a charity or cause. Note your ideas below. Work with a partner and explain how you helped.

Charity / Cause	How you helped

Last year, I volunteered at a hospital. I read books to young children.

9B I'll make a donation.

LANGUAGE FOCUS Talking about fundraising

A ▶ **9.4** Read the information. Answer these questions with a partner.

1 What two benefits of online fundraising does the infographic show?

2 According to the infographic, which online platform is the most effective way of raising money?

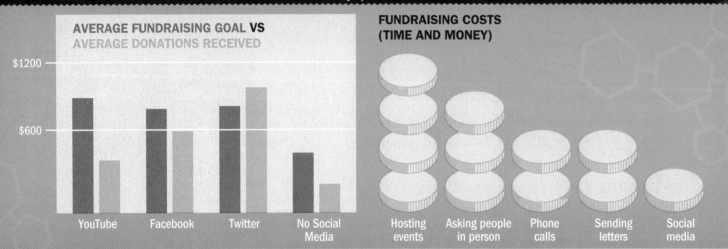

GIVING ONLINE Statistics show that fundraising online can generate more donations than traditional methods. Costs are also lower—both in terms of time and money spent.

AVERAGE FUNDRAISING GOAL VS
AVERAGE DONATIONS RECEIVED

FUNDRAISING COSTS
(TIME AND MONEY)

B ▶ **9.5** Two people are talking about fundraising. Listen and complete the sentences.

1 The man is raising money for a local _____ charity.

2 The man is using _____ to collect donations.

3 His friend says he will donate _____ dollars.

C ▶ **9.6** Watch and study the language in the chart.

Making offers and describing real conditions	
I need help planning the event.	OK. I'll help you.
I'll help you if I have enough time. I'll give you a hand if you need another person.	If I have enough time, I'll help you. If you need another person, I'll give you a hand.
We won't have enough people if you don't help.	If you don't help, we won't have enough people.
If I give $20, will you give the same amount?	Yes, I will. / No, I won't.

For more information on **will for offers and conditions**, see Grammar Summary 9 on page 157.

D Match each sentence to the offer.

1 Jill isn't here yet. ○ ○ I'll donate $20 more.

2 We're almost at our fundraising goal. ○ ○ Sure, I'll take you.

3 We need two more volunteers this weekend. ○ ○ I'll explain it to you.

4 Can someone give me a ride to the event? ○ ○ OK, I'll call her.

5 I don't understand what this charity does. ○ ○ OK, we'll come on Saturday.

E ▶ **9.7** Complete the information. Circle the correct options. Listen and check your answers.

Giving has never been easier. With the One Today app, you get details of a different charity sent to your smartphone every day. If you ¹(**decide**/**will decide**) to donate, the app ²(**is sending**/**will send**) money directly to that day's charity.

The app is customizable, too. If you ³(**add**/**will add**) details about your preferences, the app ⁴(**is sending**/**will send**) information about different charities based on your interests. Many donations are just a dollar. The app's developers feel that more people will give money if the donations ⁵(**are**/**will be**) small.

F Complete the sentences with your own ideas.

1 A: I'm thinking of volunteering at the hospital on weekends.

   B: Great! If you do, I'll _____ .

2 A: Do you think we should hold our fundraiser at 3:00 p.m. or 7:00 p.m.?

   B: Definitely at 7:00. If you hold it at 3:00, _____ .

3 A: What's the advantage of using social media to raise money for charity?

   B: If you use social media, _____ .

SPEAKING Planning an event

A Work in a group. Your school is going to hold an outdoor fundraiser for a charity of your choice. Decide on a charity and then plan the event. Discuss the questions below.

How will you advertise?   When and where will the event be held?
What activities will there be?   What will each person's responsibilities be?

B Create a backup plan in case these things happen. What will you do in each case?

It rains.   Nobody comes.   Nobody wants to donate.

If it rains, we'll have it on a different day.

Yeah, we'll try to move it to the following weekend.

9C Donation revolution

PRE-READING Predicting

A Read the lesson title. What do you think the passage is mainly about? Discuss with a partner.

B Read the passage. Check your prediction.

U.N. soldiers help evacuate Haitian children from a refugee camp after the 2010 earthquake.

▶ 9.8

1   In 2010, a huge earthquake hit Haiti, causing the deaths of over a hundred thousand people and millions of dollars' worth of **damage**. The international community jumped into action[1] to provide aid. On this occasion, funds were raised with amazing speed—within a week of the quake, the American Red Cross had raised $22 million. The reason? People were donating via their mobile phones.

2   Technological **advances** have changed how charities work. Gone are the days when someone knocked on your front door and politely asked you to make a donation. In today's world of computers, smartphones, tablets, and smartwatches, charities can now reach more people than ever before.

3   Social media in particular has had a great **impact** on charity. News of **disasters** spreads quickly around the world. This enables charities to raise money extremely quickly, as in Haiti. And the quicker aid can be delivered, the more lives can be saved. Individual fundraising has also benefited.

Most people are now so well-connected through sites like Facebook that asking people to contribute to your chosen cause is easier than ever.

4   New, **innovative** ways of donating are being thought up all the time. For example, if you want to support a good cause and keep fit at the same time, you can use an app called Charity Miles. The app can track the distance you run or cycle. For every kilometer you cover, the app's sponsors will make a donation to a charity of your choice. There's also SnapDonate, which allows users to donate simply by taking a photo of a charity's logo with their smartphone. The app recognizes the logo and allows users to immediately make a donation through their phones. This cuts out the need for entering payment details on charity websites, and makes the process of donating small amounts to multiple charities much simpler.

5   Apps like these are growing in number, and that can only be a good thing. In the future, it's likely that we'll all be giving to our favorite causes more easily and more often.

[1] **jump into action:** *v.* to act quickly

UNDERSTANDING PURPOSE

Choose the option that describes the main purpose of each paragraph.

Paragraph 1
- **a** gives an example of a relief effort that benefited from new technology.
- **b** explains how bad the Haiti earthquake was for the people there.

Paragraph 2
- **a** describes how to donate using a charity's website.
- **b** compares fundraising methods in the past with those in the present.

Paragraph 3
- **a** explains the effect social media has had on fundraising.
- **b** describes how to raise money using Facebook.

Paragraph 4
- **a** compares two new apps.
- **b** gives examples of new ways of donating.

UNDERSTANDING DETAILS

Circle **T** for true, **F** for false, or **NG** if the information is not given in the passage.

1 The 2010 Haiti earthquake was the biggest in the country's history.	**T**	**F**	**NG**
2 In 2010, the American Red Cross raised $22 million in less than one week.	**T**	**F**	**NG**
3 After the Haiti earthquake, people donated money using their mobile phones.	**T**	**F**	**NG**
4 Charities raise more money through social media than through their own websites.	**T**	**F**	**NG**
5 Charity Miles raises money for charity while you're running.	**T**	**F**	**NG**
6 SnapDonate donates money every time you take a selfie.	**T**	**F**	**NG**

BUILDING VOCABULARY

A Complete the sentences using the correct form of the words in **blue** from the passage.

1 The way charities raise money has changed due to _____ in technology.

2 Charity Miles is an example of a(n) _____ new app.

3 The 2010 Haiti earthquake is an example of a natural _____.

4 The use of new technology has had a huge _____ on the speed of fundraising.

5 Earthquakes can cause a lot of _____.

B CRITICAL THINKING

Evaluating Read paragraph four again. Which app do you think would be more effective at raising money? Discuss with a partner.

9D Should you donate differently?

TEDTALKS

JOY SUN is a **veteran** aid worker who has **dedicated** her career to helping the poor. Her idea worth spreading is that there may be more value in giving money directly to poor people, for needs the **recipients** identify themselves, rather than **investing** in aid programs.

PREVIEWING

Read the paragraph above. Match each **bold** word to its meaning. You will hear these words in the TED Talk.

1 people who receive something: _____

2 given all your time and effort to: _____

3 an experienced person: _____

4 putting money into something: _____

VIEWING

A ▶ **9.9** Watch Part 1 of the TED Talk. Check [✓] each statement that Sun agrees with.

☐ It can be a good idea to give cash directly to poor people.

☐ Aid workers do more good for poor people than they can do for themselves.

☐ Poor people are poor partly because they don't make good choices.

B ▶ **9.10** Watch Part 2 of the TED Talk. The chart shows what happened in three countries when poor people received cash. Complete the notes by circling the correct words.

Uruguay	Sri Lanka	Kenya
• Pregnant women bought better (**food / clothing**). • Women gave birth to healthier babies.	• Men invested in their (**businesses / homes**).	• People invested in a range of assets.[1] • Farming and business income (**increased / decreased**).

[1] **assets:** *n.* the things someone owns

C ▶ **9.11** Look at the graph. Does it show a successful or unsuccessful aid program? Discuss with a partner. Watch Part 3 of the talk to check your answer.

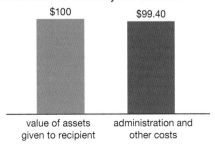

$100 $99.40

value of assets given to recipient   administration and other costs

D ▶ **9.12** Watch Part 4 of the TED Talk. Circle the correct words to complete the summary.

GiveDirectly sends [1](**food** / **money**) directly to the poor. So far the organization has helped [2](**1,000** / **35,000**) people in Kenya and Uganda. Cash is sent to families in [3](**one-time** / **monthly**) payments. The organization looks for the [4](**poorest** / **youngest**) people in the poorest places. Sun wants other aid organizations to prove they are doing more for the poor than the poor do for themselves.

A man receives cash from GiveDirectly through his mobile phone.

E CRITICAL THINKING

Reflecting Has Joy Sun's talk changed the way you think about giving to charity? Why or why not? Discuss with a partner.

VOCABULARY IN CONTEXT

▶ **9.13** Watch the excerpts from the TED Talk. Choose the correct meaning of the words.

PRESENTATION SKILLS Using supporting evidence

> In any presentation, it's important to support any points you make with evidence. For example, you could choose to:
>
> give a statistic   cite some research   tell an anecdote

A ▶ **9.14** Watch the excerpts from Joy Sun's TED Talk. Notice how Sun cites research to support her argument.

B ▶ **9.15** Watch the excerpts. Match each speaker to the type of supporting evidence they use.

1 Munir Virani   ○   ○   tells an anecdote.

2 A. J. Jacobs   ○   ○   cites some research.

3 Andras Forgacs   ○   ○   gives a statistic.

C Work in a group. Each person chooses a topic to talk about for 30 seconds. As part of your talk, use some supporting evidence.

> a good charity to support   a good place to volunteer
> something good your school does   why giving time is better than giving money

9E Choosing a charity

A boy in Aceh, Indonesia, carries aid dropped by helicopter after the 2004 Indian Ocean Tsunami.

COMMUNICATE How to give

A Six charities are asking for donations. Turn to page 143 and read the information.

B Work in a group. You have $100 to donate to one or more charities. Decide as a group who to give to, and how much to give.

> I think we should give some to Tsunami Relief.

> Maybe we should give to a local charity. It will help our community.

C Work with another group. Present your ideas. Give reasons for your decision.

Explaining reasons

Let me tell you why. *Let me explain why.* *Let me give you the reason.*

WRITING A charity I support

A Think about a cause or a charity that you support. Consider the following questions.

What does the charity do? What are donations used for? Why do you think it's a good cause?

B Use the questions above to write about the charity.

> I support the charity Sustrans. It's a charity that works to make it easier for people to travel by foot, bike, or public transportation. I think it's a great cause. If people can use their cars less, it will be good for the environment.

Presentation 3

MODEL PRESENTATION

A Complete the transcript of the presentation using the words in the box.

ate out	check out	definitely	grew up	in
lively	locally	museums	suburbs	to

Today, I'm going to tell you about a great city that I visited last year—Toronto. Toronto is the most populous city in Canada. According ¹_____ the 2011 census, Toronto had a population of around three million people and it's the fourth largest city in North America. It's a really ²_____ and cosmopolitan place. I stayed for a week with my friend Josh, who ³_____ in Toronto. He lives in the ⁴_____, but I visited the downtown area almost every day. There are so many things to do and places to see. I visited a lot of ⁵_____ and art galleries, and in the evenings I ⁶_____ at some great restaurants. Toronto is also well known for its music scene—I managed to ⁷_____ some really cool bands while I was there. My favorite place though was St. Lawrence Market. According to National Geographic, it is the world's best food market, and I could see why. You can spend hours there looking at and trying some of the ⁸_____-produced food. ⁹_____ the future, I'm hoping to visit again. When I finish university, I'd love to be able to find a job there and make Toronto my home. It ¹⁰_____ won't be easy, but who knows? Thank you so much.

B ▶ **P.3** Watch the presentation and check your answers.

C ▶ **P.3** Review the list of presentation skills from Units 1–9 below. Which does the speaker use? Check [✓] each skill used as you watch again.

The speaker …
- ☐ uses questions to signpost
- ☐ personalizes the presentation
- ☐ closes the presentation effectively
- ☐ provides background information
- ☐ numbers key points
- ☐ uses their voice effectively
- ☐ tells an anecdote
- ☐ uses supporting evidence
- ☐ uses an effective slide

YOUR TURN

A You are going to plan and give a short presentation to a partner about a city you've visited, or a city you'd like to visit. Use some or all of the questions below to make some notes.

> What's the name of the city?
>
> Where is it exactly?
>
> What's special about it?
>
> What did you do there? / What would you like to do there?

B Look at the useful phrases in the box below. Think about which ones you will need in your presentation.

Useful phrases

Places in a city:	*galleries, markets, museums, riverfront, suburbs, theaters*
Adjectives to describe a city:	*bustling, lively, modern, multicultural*
Phrasal verbs:	*eat out, check out, hang out, get around*
Future hopes:	*I'd love to ... / Hopefully, I'll ...*

C Work with a partner. Take turns giving your presentation using your notes. Use some of the presentation skills from Units 1–9. As you listen, check [✓] each skill your partner uses.

The speaker ...
- ☐ uses questions to signpost
- ☐ personalizes the presentation
- ☐ closes the presentation effectively
- ☐ provides background information
- ☐ numbers key points
- ☐ uses their voice effectively
- ☐ tells an anecdote
- ☐ uses supporting evidence
- ☐ uses an effective slide

D Give your partner some feedback on their talk. Include two things you liked, and one thing he or she can improve.

> That was really good. I liked the anecdote you told and the slides you used were good. Next time, you could try using more evidence to support what you say.

Mind and Machine

" We are really only scratching the surface of what is possible today. *"*

Tan Le
Entrepreneur, TED speaker

UNIT GOALS

In this unit, you will …

- talk about the capabilities of the human brain.

- read about new technology that you control with your mind.

- watch a TED Talk about a technology with life-changing applications.

WARM UP

▶ **10.1** Watch part of Tan Le's TED Talk. Answer the questions with a partner.

1 What does the headset allow Evan to do?

2 What do you think this technology could be used for?

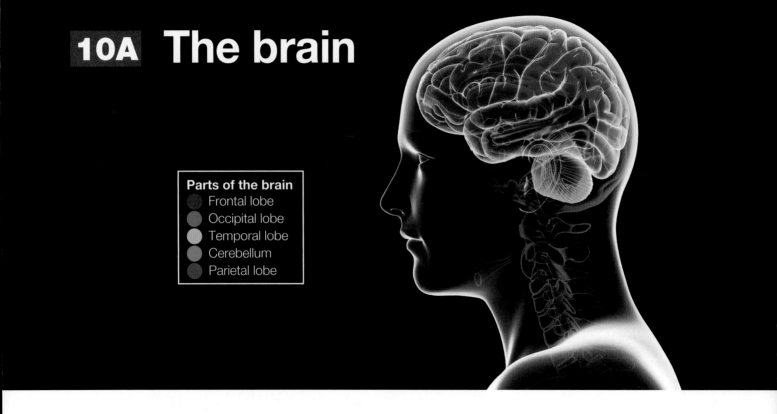

10A The brain

Parts of the brain
- Frontal lobe
- Occipital lobe
- Temporal lobe
- Cerebellum
- Parietal lobe

VOCABULARY Brain functions

A ▶ **10.2** Listen and match each part of the brain to its function.

- Frontal lobe ○   ○ long-term **memory**, understanding language
- Occipital lobe ○   ○ pain and touch **sensations**, numbers, spelling
- Temporal lobe ○   ○ **concentration**, problem-solving, **emotions**
- Cerebellum ○   ○ processing visual information, **dreams**
- Parietal lobe ○   ○ **balance**, hand-eye coordination

B Complete the sentences. Circle the correct words.

1 **Balance** is important when you (**sleep** / **walk**).

2 When you **concentrate**, you (**talk quickly** / **think hard**) about something.

3 **Dreams** are thoughts you have when you're (**asleep** / **awake**).

4 An example of an **emotion** is (**love** / **language**).

5 Your **memory** is your ability to (**create** / **remember**) things.

6 A **sensation** is a (**physical feeling** / **type of memory**).

C Work with a partner. Which parts of the brain do you think are involved in these activities?

solving a math problem	playing tennis	cooking dinner
looking at a pretty sunset	writing an essay	remembering your fifth birthday

I think solving a math problem involves the frontal lobe.

I agree. I think it also involves the …

LISTENING The power of visualization

> **Listening for instructions**
> In English, instructions are often given using the imperative form of the verb. For example:
>
> *Open your books.*   *Don't forget to ...*   *Be quiet.*

Brian Scholl, psychology professor

A ▶ **10.3** Watch psychology professor Brian Scholl describe a simple experiment. What is the aim of the experiment?

B ▶ **10.3** Watch again. Number the steps in the experiment 1–4.

_____ Try to make some baskets.

_____ Crumple up some pieces of paper.

_____ Visualize your throw and then try to make some baskets.

_____ Set up a wastebasket.

C CRITICAL THINKING

Applying Work with a partner. Try the experiment Scholl described. Discuss your results.

SPEAKING Talking about a game

A ▶ **10.4** What kind of game is the person playing on their phone?

A: Hey, what are you doing?

B: I'm playing a brain game.

A: A brain game? What's that?

B: It's an app that exercises your brain.
I use it every day. Do you want to try?   have a go / give it a go

A: Sure!   Yeah, OK. / I'd love to!

B: There are different games that exercise different parts of your brain.

A: Wow! This one's really tricky.   complicated / difficult

B: Yeah, it is at first. But keep trying. You'll   don't give up / don't quit
get better really quickly.

B Practice the conversation with a partner. Practice again using the words on the right.

C Work with a partner. Try the following brain game. Count each f in the sentence below.

Fifty-five fireflies flew from the top to the bottom of the fig tree.

Was it difficult? Can you explain why? Discuss with your partner.

D Turn to page 144 and try two more brain games. Which one do you find most difficult?

10B That's incredible!

LANGUAGE FOCUS Discussing facts

A ▶ **10.5** Read the information. Which fact do you find the most incredible?

THE INCREDIBLE BRAIN
Here are six amazing facts about our incredible brains.

 We have an average of **70,000** thoughts every day.

 The **100,000** miles of fibers that connect parts of the brain could easily circle the Earth four times.

 Your brain can't feel **pain**.

 Your brain uses **20%** of the total oxygen in your body.

 An average human brain has an estimated **100 billion** brain cells.

 The **structure** of your brain changes every time you learn something new.

B ▶ **10.6** Listen to an expert give additional information about the brain. Circle **T** for true or **F** for false.

1 Your brain can generate enough energy to power a lightbulb. **T** **F**

2 Humans only use about 10 percent of their brain. **T** **F**

3 Men's and women's brains are the same size. **T** **F**

C ▶ **10.7** Watch and study the language in the chart.

Using adverbial phrases	
Time We have an average of 70,000 thoughts every day. Your brain stops growing at age 25.	**Other examples** *a day* *after a while*
Manner Without oxygen, your brain would quickly die. The children are playing brain games quietly.	**Other examples** *slowly* *calmly*
Attitude Hopefully, tech innovations will help people with brain injuries. Fortunately, researchers are learning more and more about the brain.	**Other examples** *Luckily,* *Interestingly,*

For more information on **adverbial phrases**, see Grammar Summary 10 on page 158.

D Unscramble the sentences.

1 time / for / science / Randy / studied / a / long _____

2 ten / age / three languages / Carrie / learned / before _____

3 easily / word problems / Bianca / solve / can _____

4 the exam / unfortunately / Matt / didn't pass _____

E Circle the correct word in each sentence.

1 She solved this word puzzle so (**easy** / **easily**).

2 He thought the answer was really (**obvious** / **obviously**).

3 (**Amazing** / **Amazingly**), he memorized all the words in the book.

4 He answered all the questions (**correct** / **correctly**).

5 She's very (**good** / **well**) at doing math in her head.

6 He was (**lucky** / **luckily**) to have such an amazing brain.

F ▶ **10.8** Complete the information with words from the box. One is extra. Listen and check your answers.

at	amazingly	constantly	easily	for	in	well

Author Daniel Tammet is very good with numbers. ¹_____, he can memorize pi (π) to 22,500 digits, and he can multiply huge numbers in his head ²_____ just seconds.

For Tammet, each number has a color, shape, and texture. He says the number 1 is like a shining light, 3 is green, and 5 is like thunder.

This ability enables him to perform amazing feats quite ³_____. As Tammet explains, "When I multiply numbers together, I see two shapes. The image starts to change and evolve, and a third shape emerges."

As a child, Tammet ⁴_____ suffered from violent and painful seizures—a condition that affects the heart and brain. In spite of this, he performed extremely ⁵_____ at school. Tammet only discovered why he was different ⁶_____ age 25. Doctors diagnosed him as being an autistic savant—a person who suffers from a development disorder but who has amazing brain functions.

Daniel Tammet can multiply huge numbers in his head.

SPEAKING A logic puzzle

Work with a partner. You are going to try a logic puzzle. Turn to page 144 and follow the instructions.

A car is driven hands-free in a demonstration.

10C Power of the mind

PRE-READING Predicting

A Look at the title and skim the text quickly. What do you think the reading is mainly about?

    a the problems of using mind-control technology

    b applications of mind-control technology

B Read the passage. Check your prediction.

▶ 10.9

1   Mind control is no longer science fiction. Thanks to **breakthroughs** in our understanding of the brain, together with new technology, there are already some amazing
5   things we can do.

Thinker Thing

In 2012, a Chilean company called Thinker Thing produced the first object to be created by thought alone. The company used an electroencephalography
10   (EEG) headset together with a 3D printer. A user was shown a series of **evolving** shapes on a computer screen. The EEG headset was able to tell if the user had positive or negative responses to the shapes. Eventually, an object was printed in 3D in line with the
15   user's preferences. As this technology improves, it's possible that every child will be able to design and build their perfect toy in just minutes.

BrainDriver

In Germany, engineers have developed an
20   application called BrainDriver that allows a driver to control a car with his or her mind. The idea is to combine an EEG headset with an **autonomous** driving system. So as your car drives itself, you'll be able to make some key decisions without pressing
25   any buttons. For example, you'll be able to choose a more interesting route, speed up, or make a stop to pick up some food. All these decisions could be made using your mind and **interpreted** by the car's computer.

30   ### MiND Ensemble

At the University of Michigan, the MiND Ensemble (Music in Neural Dimensions) creates music based on a person's thoughts. A performer wears EEG headwear that records **signals** from their brain.
35   Special computer software then produces different sounds and musical notes based on these signals. So, as the person's thoughts change, so does the music. Right now, there is no guarantee that the music in your head will be the same as what the
40   computer produces, but in the future, who knows?

UNDERSTANDING MAIN IDEAS

Match the two parts of each sentence.

1 Thinker Thing ○   ○ allows someone to control a car using their mind.

2 The BrainDriver application ○   ○ makes music using people's thoughts.

3 The MiND Ensemble ○   ○ creates objects using mind control.

UNDERSTANDING DETAILS

Complete the chart. Write the letters **a–f**.

a uses an EEG headset   **b** connects to a 3D printer   **c** needs a computer

d was developed in Europe   **e** creates something new   **f** shows objects on a screen

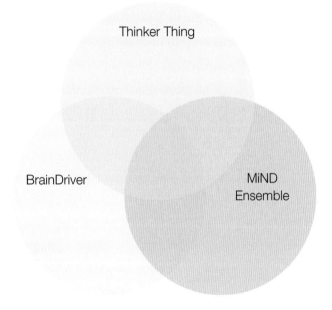

BUILDING VOCABULARY

A Circle the correct option to complete each sentence.

1 A **breakthrough** is an important (**discovery** / **decision**).

2 If something **evolves**, it (**stays the same** / **changes**).

3 If something is **autonomous**, (**no one** / **one person**) controls it.

4 If you **interpret** something, you work out the (**cause** / **meaning**) of it.

5 A **signal** is a way of sending and receiving (**information** / **objects**).

B CRITICAL THINKING

Evaluating Work with a partner. Make a list of the advantages and disadvantages of each piece of technology mentioned in the passage. Which of the applications do you think will be most common in the future?

10D A headset that reads your brainwaves

TEDTALKS

In **TAN LE**'s talk, she demonstrates a new computer **interface** that makes it possible to control **virtual** objects simply by **visualizing** their movement. Her idea worth spreading is that new technology that "reads our minds" has all kinds of life-changing **applications**, particularly for the disabled.

PREVIEWING

Read the paragraph above. Match each **bold** word to its meaning.
You will hear these words in the TED Talk.

1 existing only on computers: _____

2 uses of an idea: _____

3 creating an image in the mind: _____

4 a computer's connection to hardware: _____

VIEWING

A ▶ **10.10** Complete the summary with the words from the box. Then watch Part 1 of the TED Talk to check your answers.

body language	brain	emotions	human	light	machine

Human-to-[1]_____ **communication**

- until now, limited to conscious and direct forms, e.g., turning on a [2]_____
- people need to give a command to a machine to get it to do something

Human-to-[3]_____ **communication**

- more complex because we get information from facial expressions and [4]_____
- can also understand feelings and [5]_____ from talking to someone

Tan Le's goal

- to get computers to respond more like a person would by interpreting signals from the [6]_____

B ▶ **10.11** Watch Part 2 of the TED Talk. Number the steps (1–5) in Le's demonstration.

_____ Evan imagines an object coming forward again.

_____ The computer records how Evan thinks about "pull."

_____ Evan chooses to visualize the action "pull."

_____ Tan Le asks Evan to visualize the object coming forward for eight seconds.

_____ The object moves forward on the screen.

C ▶ **10.12** Watch Part 3 of the TED Talk. What does Le say the technology can be used for? Check [✓] each thing Le mentions.

☐ gaming   ☐ driving cars   ☐ controlling things in your house

☐ toys   ☐ education   ☐ helping people with disabilities

D CRITICAL THINKING

Evaluating What are the possible disadvantages of controlling something using your mind rather than with traditional methods? Discuss with a partner.

VOCABULARY IN CONTEXT

▶ **10.13** Watch the excerpts from the TED Talk. Choose the correct meaning of the words.

PRESENTATION SKILLS Dealing with the unexpected

> Even with a well-prepared presentation, some things may go wrong or there may be things the presenter did not expect. The best thing to do in these situations is to relax and calmly move forward. Some things that are unexpected may be positive, such as when the audience is especially responsive to your ideas.

A ▶ **10.14** Watch another part of Tan Le's TED Talk. What happened that was unexpected?

a Evan couldn't think of a word.

b Evan misunderstood the directions.

c The demo didn't seem to work well.

B ▶ **10.14** Watch the excerpt again. How did Le deal with the unexpected?

C Work in a group. What other unexpected things could happen during a presentation?

> Well, you could forget what you wanted to say.

> Or someone could interrupt you and ask a question.

10E I need that!

COMMUNICATE A new product

A Work in a group. Think about the technology that Tan Le described. Discuss some possible applications of the technology. Look at the categories below for ideas.

travel	shopping	sports	education
work	saving lives	disabilities	entertainment

B Choose one application of Tan Le's technology, and think of a new product that could make use of it. Prepare to explain what it does, how it's useful, and who should buy it. Make notes below.

> Name of product:
>
> What it does:
>
> How it's useful:
>
> Who should buy it:

> **Explaining the uses of something**
> *It's useful for ...*   *You can use it to ...*   *It's designed for ...*

C Prepare a TV commercial for your product. Write out a short script. Then act out the commercial for the class.

> Do you ever get hungry but feel too busy to make a snack?

> With Mind Delivery, you won't need to cook again. It works like this ...

WRITING A proposal

Choose one of the products you heard about above. Write an email to Tan Le asking to use her technology in your product. Explain what the product is and how it works.

> Dear Tan Le,
> I have a great idea for a product that uses your amazing new technology.
> If you're not too busy, I'd like to take some time to explain it to you. ...

118

11 Nature

Louie Schwartzberg

" Always take time to smell the flowers, and let it fill you with beauty. **"**

Louie Schwartzberg
Filmmaker, TED speaker

UNIT GOALS

In this unit, you will …

- talk about nature.
- read about the relationship between animals and plants.
- watch a TED Talk about the wonder of pollination.

WARM UP

▶ **11.1** Watch part of Louie Schwartzberg's TED Talk. Answer the questions with a partner.

1 What do you see in the video?

2 Where are the best places near you to experience nature?

A car drives along the Hana Highway, Hawaii.

11A Nature at its best

VOCABULARY Nature

A Read the information about the Hana Highway. Complete the chart with the words in **bold**.

To appreciate nature at its best, consider driving the 100-kilometer Hana Highway on the Hawaiian **island** of Maui. The road winds its way along the coast to the town of Hana. Keep an eye out for wildlife on the way. There are **birds** and beautiful wild **plants** in the **forest.** Drive it in a day, or stop at the state park to **go hiking** or **camping**.

Places in nature	Wildlife	Things to do in nature
river	animals	swim
cave	insects	go for a walk
volcano	fish	climb a mountain

B Add one more word to each category. Compare with a partner.

C How often do you spend time in nature? What do you like to do there? Discuss with a partner.

I try to go out every week. I like to just walk.

I go hiking about once a month.

LISTENING My experiences in nature

> **Noticing auxiliary verbs**
> Auxiliary verbs are often contracted and can be difficult to hear.
> For example, *I have* is usually shortened to *I've*.

Tony Gainsford

A ▶ **11.2** Watch Tony Gainsford talking about his experiences in nature. Circle the places in nature that he can enjoy near his home.

| a beach | a forest | a park | a river |

B ▶ **11.2** Watch again. Match the sentence parts to make true statements about Gainsford's experiences.

1 He's been diving in   ○   ○   Africa.

2 He saw sea turtles in   ○   ○   Australia.

3 He's never been to   ○   ○   Greece.

C **CRITICAL THINKING**

Personalizing Have you had any similar experiences to Gainsford? Discuss with a partner.

SPEAKING Talking about nature

A ▶ **11.3** Where are the two people planning to go?

A: It's great to get out and enjoy nature while   appreciate / be a part of
the weather is so nice.

B: You know, we should go to Evans National
Forest sometime.

A: That would be fun. I've never been there.
Have you?

B: Yeah, I have. It was so pretty.   breathtaking / gorgeous

A: Have you ever hiked up the mountain there?   climbed up / been to the top of

B: No, I haven't. I'd love to, though.

A: OK, we should make a plan. Hopefully, we'll
spot some deer or other wildlife.   see / find

B Practice the conversation with a partner. Practice again using the words on the right.

C Work with a partner. Think of something fun to do outside together.

> What do you think we should do?

> How about visiting the greenbelt by the river? I hear it's pretty nice.

11B Nature and you

LANGUAGE FOCUS Discussing experiences

A ▶ **11.4** Read the information. Do you think children in your country are similar? Discuss with a partner.

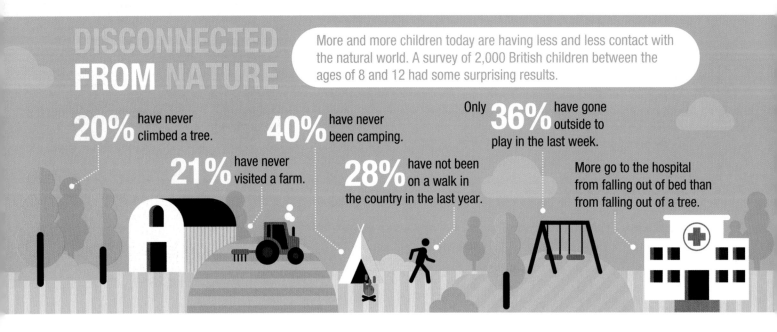

DISCONNECTED FROM NATURE

More and more children today are having less and less contact with the natural world. A survey of 2,000 British children between the ages of 8 and 12 had some surprising results.

20% have never climbed a tree.

21% have never visited a farm.

40% have never been camping.

28% have not been on a walk in the country in the last year.

Only **36%** have gone outside to play in the last week.

More go to the hospital from falling out of bed than from falling out of a tree.

B ▶ **11.5** Listen to a health expert offer some advice. Complete the suggestions.

1 Adults need to _____ for children.

2 We need to look at why children are _____ more.

3 For a few hours a week, parents shouldn't allow their children to _____ .

C ▶ **11.6** Watch and study the language in the chart.

Talking about past experiences	
Have you ever climbed a tree?	Yes, I have. I've climbed several. No, I haven't.
Has she ever been camping?	Yes, she has. She's been camping twice. No, she hasn't. She's never been camping.
Have you ever visited a farm?	Yes, I have. I visited one a few years ago. Yes, but I haven't visited one in a long time.
I've gone outside every day this week.	Me too. / I have too. Really? I haven't.
I've never swum in the ocean.	Me neither. / I haven't, either.

For more information on **present perfect**, see Grammar Summary 11 on page 158.

D ▶ **11.7** Complete the information with the correct form of the verbs in the box. Listen and check your answers.

build	connect	love	make	~~see~~	want

Have you ever ¹_____seen_____ a tree house? Have you ever ²_____ to live in one? One man has ³_____ that dream come true.

Foster Huntington has always ⁴_____ tree houses, so when he decided to move from New York City to Oregon, he had an idea: He would build his own.

He has ⁵_____ not one, but two tree houses. And he has ⁶_____ them with a bridge to create a truly unique living space high above the ground. It may not be for everyone, but for Huntington, it's the perfect home.

Foster Huntington and his treehouse

E Complete the conversations. Circle the correct words.

1 **A:** Have you ever been camping?

   B: Yes, I (**did** / **have**). I (**went** / **have been**) camping last summer.

2 **A:** (**Has** / **Have**) you ever (**swam** / **swum**) in the ocean?

   B: No, I haven't. But I (**swam** / **'ve swum**) in a river last summer.

3 **A:** (**Did you see** / **Have you seen**) any bears at your summer camp last August?

   B: No, but my brother (**saw** / **has seen**) one a couple of years ago.

SPEAKING Experiences in nature

Walk around the classroom. Find someone who answers *yes* to each question. Write their name and then ask a follow-up question.

Have you ever ...?	Name	Additional information
climbed a tree		
been camping		
visited a farm		
planted a tree		
been diving		

Have you ever climbed a tree?

Yes, I have.

When did you climb it?

A bee collects pollen from a lily flower.

11C The miracle of pollen

PRE-READING Predicting

A Read the definition. What animals do you know that help carry pollen? Discuss with a partner.

> **pollen** *n.* very fine, usually yellow, powder that is produced by a plant. It is carried to other plants of the same kind so that the plants can produce seeds.

B Read the passage. Which animals are mentioned?

▶ **11.8**

It happens countless times a day. A flower's bright petals and the smell of sweet nectar[1] **attract** a bee. The bee stops by for a quick taste, and small grains[2] of pollen stick to its body. The bee then travels to another flower of the same type and deposits the pollen as it has another meal. This is an example of animal pollination—a process vital to plant reproduction.[3]

It's not only plants that **depend on** animal pollination—humans do, too. Worldwide, approximately a thousand plants that we grow for food, spices, clothing fibers,[4] and medicine depend on it. If pollination suddenly stopped, we would have no apples, tomatoes, coffee, and many other goods.

This vital process is carried out by more than 200,000 different animal species known as *pollinators*. Flies and beetles—the original pollinators—date back 130 million years to the first flowering plants. Birds, butterflies, and ants also do their part. Even nonflying mammals help out: monkeys **tear open** flowers with their hands, accidentally spreading pollen into the air and onto their fur.

Pollinators are therefore vital, but they are also at risk. Climate change, habitat loss, and invasive predators all threaten them. The United States, for example, has lost over 50 percent of its honeybees over the past ten years. A **serious** threat facing bees is colony collapse disorder (CCD), when worker bees mysteriously **disappear** from their colony. Scientists are still trying to identify its cause.

There is a quote attributed to[5] Einstein that if bees ever disappeared, man would only have four years left to live. Whether that's true or not does not really matter, says wildlife photographer Louie Schwartzberg: The key point is that there is a real danger. "The healthiest food we need to eat," he says, "would disappear without pollinating plants. It's pretty serious."

---

[1] **nectar:** *n.* a sweet liquid produced by flowers
[2] **grain:** *n.* something (e.g., salt, sand) that is very small
[3] **reproduction:** *n.* the process by which living things produce young
[4] **fibers:** *n.* thin threads used to make cloth or ropes
[5] **attributed to:** *phrase* to regard as originating from a certain source

UNDERSTANDING GIST

Choose the best alternative title for the passage.

a The Secret Life of Bees   **b** The Importance of Pollinators   **c** The Wonder of Reproduction

UNDERSTANDING A PROCESS

How does pollination work? Complete the information using the words in the box.

body	nectar	petals	pollen	seed

- A flower with bright
  1 _____
  and a sweet smell
  attracts a bee.

- The bee lands on the
  flower and drinks its
  2 _____.

- Some pollen gets on
  the bee's
  3 _____.

- The bee lands on
  another flower and
  deposits the
  4 _____
  there.

- The flower now has what
  it needs to produce a
  5 _____,
  which will grow into a
  new plant.

UNDERSTANDING DETAILS

Circle **T** for true or **F** for false.

1 If pollination stopped, there would be no tomatoes.	**T**	**F**
2 There are more than 200,000 different types of pollinators.	**T**	**F**
3 Ants are the only nonflying pollinators.	**T**	**F**
4 Today, there are more honey bees in the United States than ever before.	**T**	**F**
5 Scientists have discovered the reason for colony collapse disorder.	**T**	**F**

BUILDING VOCABULARY

A Circle the correct words to complete the definitions.

1 If something **attracts** you, you want to be (**closer to** / **further away from**) it.

2 If you **tear** something **open**, you open it by (**pulling with your hands** / **using a knife**).

3 If you **depend on** something, you (**need** / **don't need**) it.

4 A **serious** problem is (**big** / **small**).

5 If something **disappears**, you can't (**see** / **understand**) it anymore.

B CRITICAL THINKING

Applying What could be done to protect pollinating plants? Discuss with a partner.

11D The hidden beauty of pollination

TEDTALKS

As a filmmaker, **LOUIE SCHWARTZBERG** uses **time-lapse** photography and slow-motion cameras to capture amazing images of nature. He is fascinated by the **coevolution** of plants and pollinators and believes that threats to pollinators deserve our attention. His idea worth spreading is that we will protect what we fall in love with, so we should enjoy the beauty in nature and **take care of** it.

PREVIEWING

Read the paragraph above. Circle the correct option for each sentence below.
You will hear these words in the TED Talk.

1 **Time-lapse** photography makes a (**slow action appear fast** / **fast action appear slow**).

2 **Coevolution** refers to two or more species evolving (**separately** / **together**).

3 You **take care of** something that is (**important** / **unimportant**) to you.

VIEWING

A ▶ **11.9** Watch Part 1 of the TED Talk. Choose what each **bold** word refers to.

1 ... **they** coevolved over 50 million years.	**a** flowers and pollinators	**b** birds and insects
2 To watch **them** move is a dance ...	**a** birds	**b** flowers
3 If **they** disappear, so do we.	**a** bees	**b** birds
4 ... and we need to take care of **it**.	**a** pollination	**b** nature

B ▶ **11.10** Watch Part 2 of the TED Talk. Choose what you think Schwartzberg means by each statement.

1 "So here is some nectar from my film."

   a Here are the parts that include flowers.

   b Here are some of the best parts of my film.

2 "I hope you'll drink, tweet, and plant some seeds to pollinate a friendly garden."

   a I hope you enjoy it and share it with others.

   b I hope you get inspired to plant your own garden.

3 "And always take time to smell the flowers, and let it fill you with beauty ..."

   a Take the time to appreciate the beautiful and natural things in life.

   b Take the time to walk in a beautiful park or forest to understand its relationship to you.

C CRITICAL THINKING

Applying What other things would be interesting to film with time-lapse photography? Discuss with a partner.

VOCABULARY IN CONTEXT

▶ **11.11** Watch the excerpts from the TED Talk. Choose the correct meaning of the words.

PRESENTATION SKILLS Calling others to action

> One effective way of closing a presentation is with a call to action—when the presenter calls upon the audience to act in some way. Often the presenter uses *we* or *our* to stress that we are all part of the solution.

A ▶ **11.12** Watch the excerpt. Notice how Schwartzberg says "we need to" take care of nature.

B ▶ **11.13** Do you remember what these TED speakers' calls to action were? Match. Then watch the excerpts and check your answers.

1 Munir Virani ○	○	"And I hope many more people will join me. If we all read more widely, there'd be more incentive for publishers to …"
2 Ann Morgan ○	○	"It is up to us to decide whether we want schools or parking lots, community-driven recycling projects, or …"
3 Andras Forgacs ○	○	"You can write a letter to your government and tell them that we need to focus on these very misunderstood creatures."
4 Alessandra Orofino ○	○	"We can design new materials, new products, and new facilities. We need to move past just killing animals …"

C Work in a group. What are some things that you think Schwartzberg would like to see people do to "take care of nature"?

A hummingbird feeds on the nectar of a flower, Costa Rica.

11E Getting out into nature

COMMUNICATE Nature weekend

A Work with a group. You're going to plan a camping trip for your class as part of "Nature Weekend." Decide on a suitable place to go camping. Explain why this is a good place.

B The aim of "Nature Weekend" is to get students to experience new things in nature. Work together to think of six possible activities. Include activities that your group members have never done before.

Activities

Day 1	Day 2
1 _____	1 _____
2 _____	2 _____
3 _____	3 _____

Have you ever been canoeing?

No, I haven't. That's a good idea. Let's do that.

C Join another group. Explain your plan. Answer any questions they may have.

> **Asking for more details**
> *What exactly …?*   *What kind of …?*   *Can you explain why you …?*

WRITING A blog post

Imagine your first day of Nature Weekend has just ended. Write a blog post describing your experiences and your planned activities for tomorrow.

> Nature Weekend is going really well! So far, I've planted a tree, made a campfire using sticks, and been bird watching. I've had such a great time. Tomorrow will be fun as well. In the morning, we're going to …

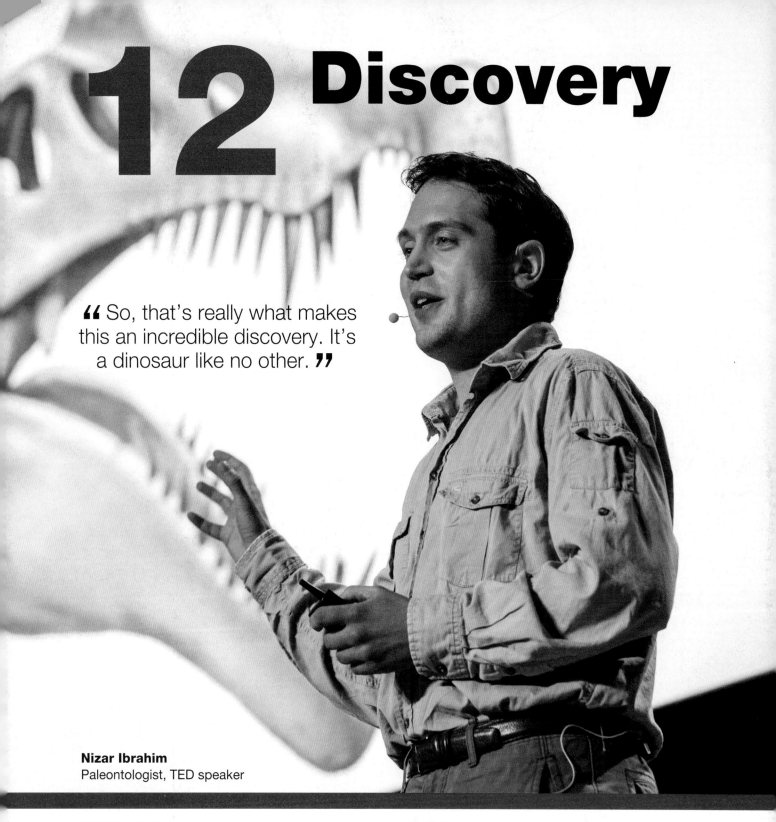

12 Discovery

" So, that's really what makes this an incredible discovery. It's a dinosaur like no other. "

Nizar Ibrahim
Paleontologist, TED speaker

UNIT GOALS

In this unit, you will ...

- talk about important discoveries.
- read about someone who is searching the world for dinosaur fossils.
- watch a TED Talk about some amazing dinosaur discoveries.

WARM UP

▶ **12.1** Watch part of Nizar Ibrahim's TED Talk. Answer the questions with a partner.

1 What dinosaurs do you know about?
2 Do you think there are many things left in the world to discover?

12A Recent discoveries

An artifact from the fifth century B.C. discovered in Lavau, France

VOCABULARY Discoveries

A Look at the photo and read the information below. Match each **bold** word to its meaning.

In 2015, archeologists **discovered** a tomb from the fifth century B.C. that is thought to belong to a Celtic prince. After **excavating** the site in Lavau, France, and **inspecting** the contents of the tomb, a number of high-quality artifacts were found.

1 digging up: _____   **2** found: _____   **3** looking at: _____

B Complete each sentence with a word from the box.

fossil	ruins	pottery	tomb	artifacts

1 The _____ of an ancient city were identified from the air.

2 Tutankhamun's _____ contained piles of gold.

3 The _____ of a five-centimeter-long ant was discovered in 2011.

4 Researchers believe the pieces of _____ were once large jars that held oil.

5 A number of valuable _____ , including several gold vases, were also found.

C Think of a museum or historical site you have visited. What did you see there? Discuss with a partner.

> I visited the Egyptian museum a few years ago. They have a lot of artifacts from the tombs of the ancient Pharaohs.

LISTENING An amazing find

Fredrik Hiebert

> **Listening for dates**
> There are different ways to say dates.
>
> March 5   *March fifth / the fifth of March*
> 1999   *nineteen ninety-nine*
> 2014   *two thousand (and) fourteen / twenty fourteen*

A ▶ **12.2** Watch archeologist Fredrik Hiebert talking about a discovery he made. What artifact did he find? Circle the correct answer.

| a vase | a key | a crown | a ring |

B ▶ **12.2** Watch again. Complete the chart.

Where was the site?	How old was the artifact?	Who did the artifact belong to?

C CRITICAL THINKING

Inferring What can we learn about the past from Hiebert's discovery? Discuss with a partner.

SPEAKING Talking about a discovery

A ▶ **12.3** How did the archeologists find the site?

A: Wow! This is interesting. Apparently, archeologists have found an ancient lost city in Honduras.   *According to this, / It says here that*

B: Really? How old is it?

A: Well, the artifacts they found there are around a thousand years old.   *about / approximately*

B: Wow! How did they find it?

A: The site was identified from the air. A team of archeologists was looking for a city known as the "City of the Monkey God." They think this is it.   *discovered / located*   *searching for / trying to find*

B: That's cool!

B Practice the conversation with a partner. Practice again using the words on the right.

C What famous discoveries can you name? They can be in any field, such as archeology, medicine, exploration, or history.

> I heard that some scientists think they have discovered a new planet in our solar system.

> I heard about that, too.

12B Amazing finds

LANGUAGE FOCUS Discussing important discoveries

A ▶ **12.4** Read the information. Which discovery do you think is most interesting? Why?

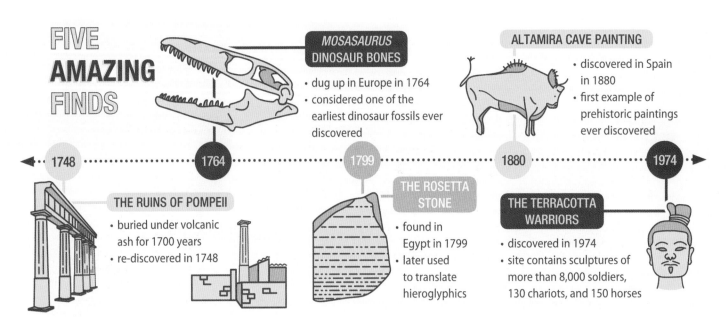

FIVE AMAZING FINDS

MOSASAURUS DINOSAUR BONES
- dug up in Europe in 1764
- considered one of the earliest dinosaur fossils ever discovered

ALTAMIRA CAVE PAINTING
- discovered in Spain in 1880
- first example of prehistoric paintings ever discovered

◀ ·· 1748 ·········· 1764 ·········· 1799 ·········· 1880 ·········· 1974 ·▶

THE RUINS OF POMPEII
- buried under volcanic ash for 1700 years
- re-discovered in 1748

THE ROSETTA STONE
- found in Egypt in 1799
- later used to translate hieroglyphics

THE TERRACOTTA WARRIORS
- discovered in 1974
- site contains sculptures of more than 8,000 soldiers, 130 chariots, and 150 horses

B ▶ **12.5** Listen to an expert giving more information about the terracotta warriors. Complete the sentences.

1 The site was a _____ built for the first emperor of China.

2 The site is over _____ years old.

3 The sculptures were originally painted in _____ colors.

C ▶ **12.6** Watch and study the language in the chart.

Talking about discoveries	
Lots of tourists visit Pompeii.	Pompeii is visited by lots of tourists.
The museum displays many artifacts.	Many artifacts are displayed by the museum.
The volcanic ash killed people instantly.	People were killed instantly by the ash.
People forgot about the city.	The city was forgotten about.
Archeologists didn't discover it until 1,700 years later.	It wasn't discovered until about 1,700 years later.
Is the cave protected?	Yes, it is.
Are the walls covered in paintings?	Yes, they are.
Was the cave found recently?	No, it wasn't. It was found over 100 years ago.
Were the animals painted in color?	Yes, they were.

For more information on **passive**, see Grammar Summary 12 on page 158.

D Rewrite each sentence as in the example.

1 They painted the cave walls in brilliant colors.

The cave walls were painted in brilliant colors.

2 They drew images of animals on the walls.

_____ .

3 They discovered the cave in Spain.

_____ .

4 They also found artifacts in the cave.

_____ .

E ▶ **12.7** Complete the information. Circle the correct options. Listen and check your answers.

The Voynich manuscript is one of the world's most mysterious books. The text [1](**writes** / **is written**) from left to right, and most pages have illustrations. The language used in the book is not known. Its alphabet [2](**contains** / **is contained**) 20–25 individual characters, and most of these [3](**made** / **are made**) using just one or two pen strokes.

Wilfrid Voynich — a Polish book dealer — [4](**discovered** / **was discovered**) the book in 1912, and it [5](**names** / **is named**) after him. Carbon dating shows that it [6](**created** / **was created**) in the early 15th century.

People have many questions about the manuscript. Some claim a microscope [7](**needed** / **was needed**) to draw some of the illustrations, but the microscope

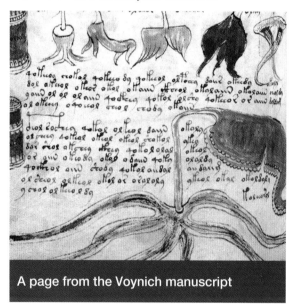

A page from the Voynich manuscript

[8](**didn't invent** / **wasn't invented**) until the 16th century. Others say the dating is not accurate, and argue that it's a modern fake.

F Complete the conversations with the correct form of the words in parentheses.

1 A: Who _____ (discover) the first dinosaur fossil?

   B: I'm not sure, but I think it _____ (find) in Europe somewhere.

2 A: Where _____ the Rosetta Stone _____ (locate) today?

   B: In the British Museum. It _____ (see) by 2.5 million people a year.

3 A: _____ King Tut _____ (bury) with a lot of valuable objects?

   B: Yes. After his tomb was opened, everything _____ (remove) and placed in a museum.

SPEAKING Discovery quiz

Work with a partner. You are going to take a short quiz about some of the world's most important discoveries. **Student A:** turn to page 143; **Student B:** turn to page 145.

Nizar Ibrahim examines fossils found in the Sahara desert.

12C The dinosaur hunter

PRE-READING Skimming

A Read the introduction to the interview. Work with a partner. Think of three questions you'd like to ask paleontologist, Nizar Ibrahim.

B Skim the passage. Which of your questions were answered?

▶ **12.8**

ike many kids, paleontologist[1] Nizar Ibrahim had a fascination with dinosaurs. He has spent most of his life searching for their fossils.

What inspired you to dedicate your life to your work?

As a child, I was always interested in animals. I was five when I received my first book about dinosaurs, and it inspired me to want to write a book of my own. When I was told that I would have to study hard and get a Ph.D., I wrote my name under the author's and added the word *Dr.* in front of it. I made the decision then and there that I would become a paleontologist.

I am so inspired by the history of life on our planet. And I feel that paleontology is our best tool to understand it.

What has been your most memorable experience in the field?

It is difficult to choose one particular memorable experience. Locating and unearthing the largest dinosaur bone ever found in the Kem Kem region of southeastern Morocco was a thrilling experience.

There is a real **buildup** of excitement when searching for fossils because most finds begin as small bits of bone, and the element of discovery and surprise is ever present.

What about the challenges?

The challenges I face during my fieldwork are very **diverse** and range from **violent** sandstorms and extensive flooding to working in the middle of the Sahara in 50°C heat.

Several years ago, I led a small expedition to the Sahara, on a very restrictive[2] budget, with just one vehicle and extremely limited supplies, which turned out to be one of the most challenging trips.

What advice would you give your younger self?

First: Follow your dreams, and don't let anyone take them away from you. Second: Don't be **discouraged**. Hurdles and **obstacles** are a part of life and can be overcome. Third: Make big plans.

[1] **paleontologist:** *n.* a scientist who studies fossils

[2] **restrictive:** *adj.* preventing someone from doing what they want to do

UNDERSTANDING GIST

Check [✓] the topics that are discussed in the passage.

☐ why Ibrahim became a paleontologist   ☐ extreme weather Ibrahim has faced

☐ an experience Ibrahim found thrilling   ☐ advice Ibrahim received as a child

UNDERSTANDING DETAILS

Are the following statements true, false, or not given according to the passage?
Circle **T** for true, **F** for false, or **NG** for not given.

1 Ibrahim was interested in animals from a young age.	**T**	**F**	**NG**
2 Ibrahim's uncle was a paleontologist.	**T**	**F**	**NG**
3 Ibrahim decided he wanted to be a paleontologist when he was a teenager.	**T**	**F**	**NG**
4 Ibrahim found a huge dinosaur bone in Morocco.	**T**	**F**	**NG**
5 Ibrahim made an amazing discovery in the Sahara.	**T**	**F**	**NG**

UNDERSTANDING REFERENTS

Read the excerpts from the passage. What do the **bold** words refer to? Circle the correct option

1 "… **it** inspired me to want to write a book of my own."

    a receiving a book about dinosaurs   **b** meeting a famous author

2 "[I] added the word Dr. in front of **it**."

    a the author's name   **b** his own name

3 "Don't let anyone take **them** away from you."

    a your discoveries   **b** your dreams

4 "… **which** turned out to be one of the most challenging trips."

    a a trip to Morocco   **b** a trip to the Sahara

BUILDING VOCABULARY

A Complete each sentence with the correct form of a word in **blue** from the passage.

1 If you feel less determined or confident about something, you feel _____ .

2 A(n) _____ storm is one that is strong and powerful.

3 A person with very _____ interests is interested in many different things.

4 A(n) _____ is something that makes it difficult to do something.

5 A(n) _____ is a gradual increase in something.

B CRITICAL THINKING

Applying What do you think would be the most challenging aspect of being a paleontologist? Discuss with a partner.

12D How we unearthed the *Spinosaurus*

TEDTALKS

NIZAR IBRAHIM's **quest** to find dinosaur fossils has taken him to extreme corners of the planet. In the Sahara, he discovered the **remains** of a **bizarre** but beautiful creature. His idea worth spreading is that there will always be amazing discoveries and adventures for paleontologists, archeologists, and other explorers.

PREVIEWING

A Read the paragraph above. Circle the correct option for each sentence below. You will hear these words in the TED Talk.

1 A **quest** is (**an unexpected discovery** / **a long search for something**).

2 The **remains** of a dinosaur might include its (**bones** / **footprints**).

3 Something that is **bizarre** is very (**difficult to find** / **strange or unusual**).

B Look at the dinosaur on page 137. What can you learn about it from the illustration?

VIEWING

A ▶ **12.9** Watch Part 1 of the TED Talk. What did Ibrahim already know about *Spinosaurus*? Complete the notes.

- Some [1]_____ were discovered 100 years ago in Egypt but were destroyed in World War II.
- *Spinosaurus* lived about [2]_____ years ago.
- From drawings, we know it was big, had a sail on its [3]_____, and a long jaw like a [4]_____.
- It probably ate [5]_____.

B ▶ **12.10** Watch Part 2 of the TED Talk. What did Ibrahim discover about *Spinosaurus* from the bones that were found? Circle the correct words.

1 *Spinosaurus*'s head was very (**different from** / **similar to**) other predatory dinosaurs.

2 *Spinosaurus*'s feet were similar in appearance to a (**cat's** / **duck's**) feet.

3 The structure of *Spinosaurus*'s bones suggests it spent a lot of time (**walking** / **in the water**).

4 *Spinosaurus* was (**bigger** / **smaller**) than a *T. rex*.

C ▶ **12.11** Watch Part 3 of the TED Talk. Ibrahim quotes dinosaur hunter Roy Chapman Andrews when he says, "Always, there has been an adventure just around the corner—and the world is still full of corners." What does he mean by this?

D CRITICAL THINKING

Analyzing What kind of things do you think we will never know about the Spinosaurus? Why not? Discuss with a partner.

VOCABULARY IN CONTEXT

▶ **12.12** Watch the excerpts from the TED Talk. Choose the correct meaning of the words.

PRESENTATION SKILLS Using descriptive language

A good presenter uses descriptive language to "paint a picture." One way to do this is to compare something to another thing the audience already knows so that they're easier to imagine.

A ▶ **12.13** Watch the excerpt. Notice the descriptive language Ibrahim uses. Which animal does he compare the *Spinosaurus*'s head to?

B ▶ **12.14** Now watch three other TED speakers. Complete the sentences.

1 Jarrett Krosoczka says a two-year-old's birthday cake is like a _____.

2 Munir Virani says that vultures are our natural _____ collectors.

3 Louie Schwartzberg compares footage of time-lapse flowers to a _____.

C Work with a partner. Describe the picture on page 127. Use descriptive language.

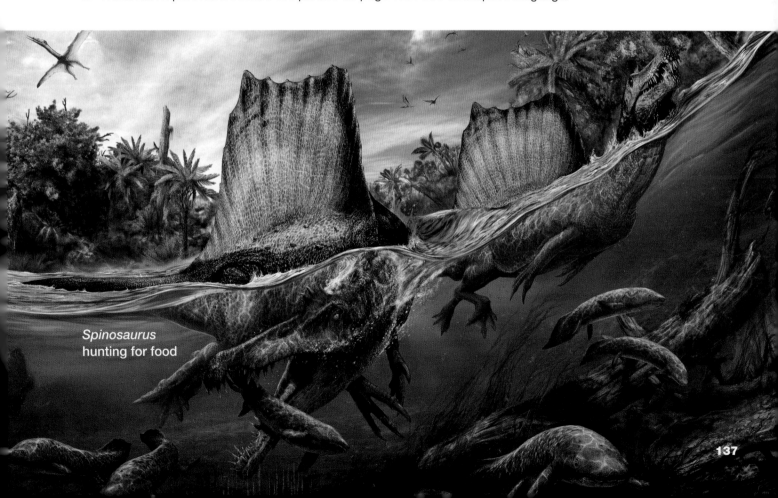

Spinosaurus
hunting for food

Archeologists discover a hand ax dating back 500,000 years.

12E A local discovery

COMMUNICATE A newspaper interview

A Work with a partner. Read the information below. Then try the roleplay.

Student A: You are an archeologist. Turn to page 145.

Student B: You are a newspaper reporter. Student A recently found some unusual items in the ground. You are going to interview him or her about the discovery. Prepare questions to ask.

What?	*How old?*
Where?	*Importance?*
When?	*... ?*

Explaining possibilities
It's possible that ...   It could be that ...   There's a possibility that ...

B Switch roles. **Student B**: Turn to page 146. **Student A**: Prepare questions to ask.

WRITING A news report

A Use the information you learned above to write a short news report.

> A mysterious skull was discovered last weekend in the backyard of a local family. Lisa Morgan, a student at Mason College, was planting a tree behind her house when she made the discovery.

B You are about to go on live TV to report your story. Read your news report to a partner.

Presentation 4

MODEL PRESENTATION

A Complete the transcript of the presentation using the words in the box.

amazingly	discovered	first	fossils	has been
has eaten	have been	hopefully	internationally	was created

Today, I want to tell you about an amazing discovery that was made not so long ago. Take a look at this picture. This is Hang Son Doong—the world's largest cave. I ¹_____ heard about this place when I saw an unbelievable video of it on YouTube. Hang Son Doong is in Vietnam. Its name means "Mountain River Cave." How big is it? Well, it's more than 5 kilometers long, 200 meters high, and 150 meters wide. In some places the cave is big enough to fit a jumbo jet inside! The cave ²_____ by a river which ³_____ away the limestone of the Annamite Mountains. How was it ⁴_____? Well, ⁵_____, nobody knew about this place until a local man named Ho Khanh found it by accident in 1991. And it was only in 2009 that the cave became ⁶_____ known after a group of British scientists went there to study it. Inside the cave, entire forests stretch out across the cave floor, and 300-million-year-old ⁷_____ have been found inside. The cave is so large it even has its own weather system. Very few people ⁸_____ inside the cave although it ⁹_____ open to the public since 2013. ¹⁰_____, I'll get the chance to go there myself one day. It looks like a truly incredible place.

B ▶ **P.4** Watch the presentation and check your answers.

C ▶ **P.4** Review the list of presentation skills from Units 1–12 below. Which does the speaker use? Check [✓] each skill used as you watch again.

The speaker …
- ☐ uses questions to signpost
- ☐ personalizes the presentation
- ☐ closes the presentation effectively
- ☐ provides background information
- ☐ numbers key points
- ☐ uses their voice effectively
- ☐ tells an anecdote
- ☐ uses supporting evidence
- ☐ uses an effective slide
- ☐ uses descriptive language
- ☐ gives a call to action
- ☐ thanks the audience

YOUR TURN

A You are going to plan and give a short presentation to a partner about an amazing discovery. Do some research and make notes using some or all of the questions below.

> What was the discovery?
>
> Where was it discovered?
>
> How was it discovered?
>
> What did people learn from it?

B Look at the useful phrases in the box below. Think about which ones you will need in your presentation.

Useful phrases

Discoveries:	*fossil, ruins, pottery, tomb, artifacts*
	find, discover, excavate, inspect
Places in nature:	*river, cave, volcano, island, forest*
Adverbial phrases:	*amazingly, incredibly, unexpectedly*
Talking about findings:	*We now know that ... / It was discovered that ...*
	We can now be sure that ...

C Work with a partner. Take turns giving your presentation using your notes. Use some of the presentation skills from Units 1–12. As you listen, check [✓] each skill your partner uses.

The speaker …
- ☐ uses questions to signpost
- ☐ personalizes the presentation
- ☐ closes the presentation effectively
- ☐ provides background information
- ☐ numbers key points
- ☐ uses their voice effectively

- ☐ tells an anecdote
- ☐ uses supporting evidence
- ☐ uses an effective slide
- ☐ uses descriptive language
- ☐ gives a call to action
- ☐ thanks the audience

D Give your partner some feedback on their talk. Include two things you liked, and one thing he or she can improve.

> Well done! You used some great descriptive language and I thought you used evidence well. Next time try and provide a bit more background information.

Communication Activities

1B SPEAKING

STUDENT A

A Look at this information about the Bengal tiger. Ask Student B questions to complete the chart.

Bengal tiger

Where do Bengal tigers live?

They live in …

Who are local police arresting?

They are arresting …

- **Population** 2,800
- **Where they live** _____
- **Conservation status** _____
- **Reason** _____

How people are helping
- Local police are arresting _____.
- Tour companies are offering _____.
- Park rangers are receiving additional training.

B Answer Student B's questions about the kiwi.

Kiwi

- **Population** 50,000–60,000
- **Where they live** New Zealand
- **Conservation status** threatened
- **Reason** habitat loss and predators such as cats and rats

How people are helping
- Scientists are increasing bird numbers through breeding programs.
- People are building fences to keep predators away.
- Volunteers are removing eggs from the wild and then returning the birds to the wild.

1E COMMUNICATE

STUDENT A

Indian python

Status
near threatened

Why are numbers declining?
hunting, human conflict

Why do they need saving?
- They help control pests such as rats and rabbits.
- They help keep diseases from rats spreading.

Something to consider
It is extremely rare for an Indian python to attack a human.

2E COMMUNICATE

STUDENT A

Alice is Steve's wife.
Pam is Steve's daughter.
Rex is Cindy's husband.
Susan is Cindy's daughter.
Max is Maggie's husband.
Cindy is Maggie's mother-in-law.
Cindy is John's daughter.
Max is John's grandson.

1B SPEAKING

STUDENT B

A Answer Student A's questions about the Bengal tiger.

Bengal tiger

- **Population** 2,800
- **Where they live** India, Nepal, Bangladesh
- **Conservation status** endangered
- **Reason** poaching and habitat loss

How people are helping
- Local police are arresting more poachers.
- Tour companies are offering trips to see them in the wild.
- Park rangers are receiving additional training.

B Look at this information about the kiwi. Ask Student A questions to complete the chart.

> Where do kiwis live?

> They live in …

> How are scientists increasing bird numbers?

> They're increasing bird numbers through …

Kiwi

- **Population** 50,000–60,000
- **Where they live** _____
- **Conservation status** _____
- **Reason** _____

How people are helping
- Scientists are increasing bird numbers through _____.
- People are building _____ to keep predators away.
- Volunteers are removing eggs from the wild and then returning the birds to the wild.

1E COMMUNICATE

STUDENT B

Frégate Island beetle

Status
critically endangered

Why are numbers declining?
natural disasters, habitat loss

Why do they need saving?
- They are unique because they only live on one two-square-kilometer island.
- They are critically endangered and could become extinct very soon without help.

Something to consider
Humans have only recently started living on their island in the Indian Ocean.

2E COMMUNICATE

STUDENT B

Rex is Alice's son.
Susan is Alice's granddaughter.
Cindy is Mike's sister.
Rex is Mike's brother-in-law.
Jessica is Steve's sister.
Alice is Jessica's sister-in-law.
John is Becky's husband.
Susan is Becky's granddaughter.

9E COMMUNICATE

CHARITY APPEALS		
Books for Good is seeking donations. If you donate $5, we will provide 10 textbooks to local schoolchildren in need. If you donate $10, we will send 20 textbooks and a dictionary. Please help!	After the recent storm that hit a South Pacific island, **Tsunami Relief** is asking for cash donations to help clothe and feed residents. Donate whatever you can—$20, $40, or more.	Help **Trees Trees Trees** replant City Park after the recent fire. If you donate $20, we will plant a tree in your name. We are also looking for volunteers to help with the planting.
The downtown **City Square Homeless Center** is asking for donations to help buy food for the homeless. We will be at City Square this weekend collecting donations. See you there!	People in deserts around the world need more freshwater. If you donate $60, a village will use the money to buy local materials to build a well. Contact the charity **Well Wishers** to make a direct donation to a village.	The Panamanian Golden Frog is nearly extinct because of disease. **Frog Friends** is asking for donations to fund research and find ways to reintroduce the frogs into the wild.

12B SPEAKING

STUDENT A

Read each question and the three choices to your partner. Mark your partner's guesses. Then see how many questions your partner got correct. (Correct answers are in **bold**.)

1 Easter Island is famous for its large statues. Where is Easter Island?

　a the Indian Ocean　　**b** the Atlantic Ocean　　**c the Pacific Ocean**

2 When were the pyramids of Egypt built?

　a 6000 B.C.　　**b 2700 B.C.**　　**c** 100 A.D.

3 Where is Machu Picchu located?

　a Peru　　**b** Egypt　　**c** Italy

4 What volcano was Pompeii built next to?

　a Vesuvius　　**b** Etna　　**c** Krakatoa

5 Where were the earliest human fossils found?

　a in Europe　　**b in Africa**　　**c** in Asia

10B SPEAKING

Try the logic puzzle below with a partner. Read the sentences and complete the results table.

1 John finished ahead of the English swimmer.

2 Roger swam well and won the race easily.

3 Surprisingly, Paul, at age 37, finished ahead of the eighteen-year-old swimmer.

4 Mark was the youngest swimmer.

5 The Australian swimmer was 32 years old.

6 There was one swimmer from New Zealand.

7 A twenty-seven-year-old finished in third place.

8 The South African swimmer was younger than Paul.

Men's 100m Freestyle – Final Standings

Position	Name	Age	Country
1			
2			
3			
4			

1E COMMUNICATE

STUDENT C

Bluefin tuna

Status
endangered

Why are numbers declining?
popularity as food, overfishing

Why do they need saving?
• Bluefin tuna are predators. They keep smaller fish numbers in check.
• Sharks feed on bluefin tuna. Fewer tuna would mean fewer sharks.

Something to consider
It's illegal to hunt bluefin tuna in many places, but many people still do.

2E COMMUNICATE

STUDENT C

Rex is Pam's brother.
Cindy is Pam's sister-in-law.
Max is Susan's brother.
Pam is Susan's aunt.
Steve is Tom's son.
Rex is Tom's grandson.
Becky is Ed's daughter.
Susan is Ed's great-granddaughter.

10A SPEAKING

Try the brain games below with a partner. Do you find them easy or difficult?

1 Say the color of each word. Do not read the word itself.

red **blue** green black **orange** blue **white** **yellow** **pink**

2 How many squares can you see?

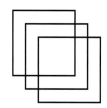

12B SPEAKING

STUDENT B

Read each question and the three choices to your partner. Mark your partner's guesses.
Then see how many questions your partner got correct. (Correct answers are in **bold**)

1 When did Christopher Columbus first visit the Americas?

    a 1492   **b** 1522   **c** 1576

2 When was the wreck of *Titanic* found?

    a 1985   **b** 1997   **c** 2005

3 When was the dwarf planet Pluto discovered?

    a 1850   **b 1930**   **c** 1990

4 What was painted on the walls of the Altamira cave?

    a writing   **b** a map   **c hunters and animals**

5 Besides hieroglyphics, what other language was included on the Rosetta Stone?

    a English   **b Greek**   **c** French

12E COMMUNICATE

STUDENT A

Look at the photo below. You and your team of archeologists recently found this artifact in the ground.
Student B is going to interview you about your discovery. Use your imagination and prepare notes to answer
any questions. Use the prompts below to help.

What exactly is it?

When / Where was it discovered?

How old is it?

Why is it important?

12E COMMUNICATE

STUDENT B

Look at the photo below. You and your team of archeologists recently found this artifact in the ground. Student A is going to interview you about your discovery. Use your imagination and prepare notes to answer any questions. Use the prompts below to help.

What exactly is it?

When / Where was it discovered?

How old is it?

Why is it important?

1E COMMUNICATE

STUDENT D

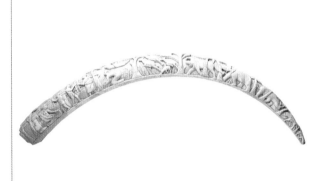

Marine iguana

Status
vulnerable

Why are numbers declining?
introduced predators, loss of nesting areas

Why do they need saving?
• They are the only iguanas that swim, so scientists have a lot to learn about them.
• Humans introduced their predators, so we have a responsibility to protect them.

Something to consider
Many tourists go to the Galapagos Islands to see them and other unique species.

2E COMMUNICATE

STUDENT D

Cindy is Rex's wife.
Max is Rex's son.
Mike is Max's uncle.
Susan is Max's sister.
Tom is Lucy's husband.
Alice is Lucy's daughter-in-law.
Ed is Carol's husband.
Cindy is Carol's granddaughter.

5A SPEAKING

A piece of furniture at the Milan International Furniture Fair

A couch on display at the Museum of Decorative Arts, Paris

2E COMMUNICATE

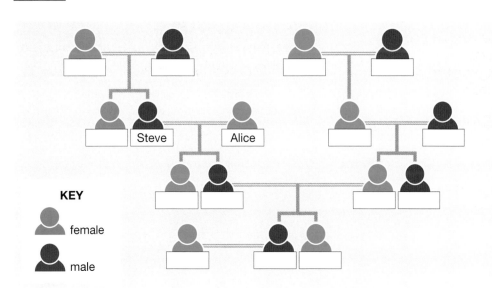

KEY

female

male

Steve

Alice

TED Talk Transcripts

Unit 1 Munir Virani: Why I love vultures

Part 1

I would like to talk to you about a very special group of animals. There are 10,000 species of birds in the world. Vultures are amongst the most threatened group of birds. When you see a vulture like this, the first thing that comes to your mind is, these are disgusting, ugly, greedy creatures that are just after your flesh, associated with politicians. I want to change that perception. I want to change those feelings you have for these birds, because they need our sympathy. They really do. And I'll tell you why.

First of all, why do they have such a bad press? When Charles Darwin went across the Atlantic in 1832 on the Beagle, he saw the turkey vulture, and he said, "These are disgusting birds with bald scarlet heads that are formed to revel in putridity." You could not get a worse insult, and that from Charles Darwin. You know, he changed his mind when he came back, and I'll tell you why. They've also be associated with Disney—personified as goofy, dumb, stupid characters.

[…] So there's two types of vultures in this planet. There are the New World vultures that are mainly found in the Americas, like the condors and the caracaras, and then the Old World vultures, where we have 16 species. From these 16, 11 of them are facing a high risk of extinction.

So why are vultures important? First of all, they provide vital ecological services. They clean up. They're our natural garbage collectors. They clean up carcasses right to the bone. They help to kill all the bacteria. They help absorb anthrax that would otherwise spread and cause huge livestock losses and diseases in other animals. Recent studies have shown that in areas where there are no vultures, carcasses take up to three to four times to decompose, and this has huge ramifications for the spread of diseases.

Part 2

So what is the problem with vultures? We have eight species of vultures that occur in Kenya, of which six are highly threatened with extinction. […] In South Asia, in countries like India and Pakistan, four species of vultures are listed as critically endangered, which means they have less than 10 or 15 years to go extinct,

[…] So what's being done? Well, we're conducting research on these birds. We're putting transmitters on them. We're trying to determine their basic ecology, and see where they go. We can see that they travel different countries, so if you focus on a problem locally, it's not going to help you. We need to work with governments in regional levels. We're working with local communities. We're talking to them about appreciating vultures, about the need from within to appreciate these wonderful creatures and the services that they provide.

How can you help? You can become active, make noise. You can write a letter to your government and tell them that we need to focus on these very misunderstood creatures. Volunteer your time to spread the word. Spread the word. When you walk out of this room, you will be informed about vultures, but speak to your families, to your children, to your neighbors about vultures.

They are very graceful. Charles Darwin said he changed his mind because he watched them fly effortlessly without energy in the skies. Kenya, this world, will be much poorer without these wonderful species. Thank you very much.

Unit 2 A. J. Jacobs: The world's largest family reunion

Part 1

Six months ago, I got an email from a man in Israel who had read one of my books, and the email said, "You don't know me, but I'm your 12th cousin." And it said, "I have a family tree with 80,000 people on it, including you, Karl Marx, and several European aristocrats."

[…] So this email inspired me to dive into genealogy, which I always thought was a very staid and proper field, but it turns out it's going through a fascinating revolution, and a controversial one. Partly, this is because of DNA and genetic testing, but partly, it's because of the Internet. There are sites that now take the Wikipedia approach to family trees, collaboration and crowdsourcing, and what you do is, you load your family tree on, and then these sites search to see if the A. J. Jacobs in your tree is the same as the A. J. Jacobs in another tree, and if it is, then you can combine, and then you combine and combine and combine until you get these massive, mega-family trees with thousands of people on them, or even millions. I'm on something on Geni called the world family tree, which has no less than a jaw-dropping 75 million people. So that's 75 million people connected by blood or marriage, sometimes both. It's in all seven continents, including Antarctica. I'm on it. Many of you are on it, whether you know it or not, and you can see the links. Here's my cousin Gwyneth Paltrow. She has no idea I exist, but we are officially cousins. We have just 17 links between us. And there's my cousin Barack Obama. And he is my aunt's fifth great-aunt's husband's father's wife's seventh great-nephew, so practically my older brother.

[…] Now, I'm not boasting, because all of you have famous people and historical figures in your tree, because we are all connected, and 75 million may seem like a lot, but in a few years, it's quite likely we will have a family tree with all, almost all, seven billion people on Earth. But does it really matter? What's the importance?

Part 2

First, it's got scientific value. This is an unprecedented history of the human race, and it's giving us valuable data about how diseases are inherited, how people migrate, and there's a team of scientists at MIT right now studying the world family tree.

Number two, it brings history alive. I found out I'm connected to Albert Einstein, so I told my seven-year-old son that, and he was totally engaged. Now Albert Einstein is not some dead white guy with weird hair. He's Uncle Albert.

[…] Number three, interconnectedness. We all come from the same ancestor, […] so that means we literally all are biological cousins as well, and estimates vary, but probably the farthest cousin you have on Earth is about a 50th cousin. Now, it's not just ancestors we share, descendants. If you have kids, and they have kids, look how quickly the descendants accumulate. So in 10, 12 generations, you're going to have thousands of offspring, and millions of offspring.

Number four, a kinder world. Now, I know that there are family feuds. I have three sons, so I see how they fight. But I think that there's also a human bias to treat your family a little better than strangers. I think this tree is going to be bad news for bigots, because they're going to have to realize that they are cousins with thousands of people in whatever ethnic group they happen to have issues with, and I think you look back at history, and a lot of the terrible things we've done to each other is because one group thinks another group is sub-human, and you can't do that anymore. We're not just part of the same species. We're part of the same family. We share 99.9 percent of our DNA.

Part 3

So I have all these hundreds and thousands, millions of new cousins. I thought, what can I do with this information? And that's when I decided, why not throw a party? So that's what I'm doing. And you're all invited. Next year, next summer, I will be hosting what I hope is the biggest and best family reunion in history. Thank you. I want you there. I want you there. It's going to be at the New York Hall of Science, which is a great venue,

[...] There's going to be exhibits and food, music. Paul McCartney is 11 steps away, so I'm hoping he brings his guitar. He hasn't RSVP'd yet, but fingers crossed. And there is going to be a day of speakers, of fascinating cousins.

[…] And, of course, the most important is that you, I want you guys there, and I invite you to go to GlobalFamilyReunion.org and figure out how you're on the family tree, because these are big issues, family and tribe, and I don't know all the answers, but I have a lot of smart relatives, including you guys, so together, I think we can figure it out. Only together can we solve these big problems. So from cousin to cousin, I thank you. I can't wait to see you. Goodbye.

Unit 3 Ann Morgan: My year reading a book from every country

Part 1

It's often said that you can tell a lot about a person by looking at what's on their bookshelves. What do my bookshelves say about me? Well, when I asked myself this question a few years ago, I made an alarming discovery. I'd always thought of myself as a fairly cultured, cosmopolitan sort of person. But my bookshelves told a rather different story. Pretty much all the titles on them were by British or North American authors, and there was almost nothing in translation. Discovering this massive, cultural blind spot in my reading came as quite a shock.

And when I thought about it, it seemed like a real shame. I knew there had to be lots of amazing stories out there by writers working in languages other than English. And it seemed really sad to think that my reading habits meant I would probably never encounter them. So, I decided to prescribe myself an intensive course of global reading. 2012 was set to be a very international year for the UK; it was the year of the London Olympics. And so I decided to use it as my time frame to try to read a novel, short story collection or memoir from every country in the world. And so I did. And it was very exciting and I learned some remarkable things and made some wonderful connections that I want to share with you today.

Part 2

So how on earth was I going to read the world? I was going to have to ask for help. So in October 2011, I registered my blog, ayearofreadingtheworld.com, and I posted a short appeal online. I explained who I was, how narrow my reading had been, and I asked anyone who cared to to leave a message suggesting what I might read from other parts of the planet. Now, I had no idea whether anyone would be interested, but within a few hours of me posting that appeal online, people started to get in touch. At first, it was friends and colleagues. Then it was friends of friends. And pretty soon, it was strangers.

Four days after I put that appeal online, I got a message from a woman called Rafidah in Kuala Lumpur. She said she loved the sound of my project, could she go to her local English-language bookshop and choose my Malaysian book and post it to me? I accepted enthusiastically, and a few weeks later, a package arrived containing not one, but two books—Rafidah's choice from Malaysia, and a book from Singapore that she had also picked out for me. Now, at the time, I was amazed that a stranger more than 6,000 miles away would go to such lengths to help someone she would probably never meet.

But Rafidah's kindness proved to be the pattern for that year. Time and again, people went out of their way to help me. Some took on research on my behalf, and others made detours on holidays and business trips to go to bookshops for me. It turns out, if you want to read the world, if you want to encounter it with an open mind, the world will help you.

Part 3

The books I read that year opened my eyes to many things. As those who enjoy reading will know, books have an extraordinary power to take you out of yourself and into someone else's mindset, so that, for a while at least, you look at the world through different eyes. That can be an uncomfortable experience, particularly if you're reading a book from a culture that may have quite different values to your own. But it can also be really enlightening. Wrestling with unfamiliar ideas can help clarify your own thinking. And it can also show up blind spots in the way you might have been looking at the world.

When I looked back at much of the English-language literature I'd grown up with, for example, I began to see quite how narrow a lot of it was, compared to the richness that the world has to offer. And as the pages turned, something else started to happen, too. Little by little, that long list of countries that I'd started the year with, changed from a rather dry, academic register of place names into living, breathing entities.

Now, I don't want to suggest that it's at all possible to get a rounded picture of a country simply by reading one book. But cumulatively, the stories I read that year made me more alive than ever before to the richness, diversity and complexity of our remarkable planet. It was as though the world's stories and the people who'd gone to such lengths to help me read them had made it real to me. These days, when I look at my bookshelves or consider the works on my e-reader, they tell a rather different story. It's the story of the power books have to connect us across political, geographical, cultural, social, religious divides. It's the tale of the potential human beings have to work together.

[…] And I hope many more people will join me. If we all read more widely, there'd be more incentive for publishers to translate more books, and we would all be richer for that.

Thank you.

Unit 4 Daria van den Bercken: Why I take the piano on the road … and in the air

Part 1

Recently, I flew over a crowd of thousands of people in Brazil playing music by George Frideric Handel. I also drove along the streets of Amsterdam, again playing music by this same composer. Let's take a look.

[Music: George Frideric Handel, "Allegro." Performed by Daria van den Bercken.]

[Video] Daria van den Bercken: I live there on the third floor. [In Dutch] I live there on the corner. I actually live there, around the corner … and you'd be really welcome.

Man: [In Dutch] Does that sound like fun?

Child: [In Dutch] Yes!

Daria van den Bercken: All this was a real magical experience for hundreds of reasons. Now you may ask, why have I done these things? They're not really typical for a musician's day-to-day life. Well, I did it because I fell in love with the music and I wanted to share it with as many people as possible.

It started a couple of years ago. I was sitting at home on the couch with the flu and browsing the Internet a little, when I found out that Handel had written works for the keyboard. Well, I was surprised. I did not know this. So I downloaded the sheet music and started playing. And what happened next was that I entered this state of pure, unprejudiced amazement. It was an experience of being totally in awe of the music, and I had not felt that in a long time. It might be easier to relate to this when you hear it. The first piece that I played through started like this. [Music] Well this sounds very melancholic, doesn't it? And I turned the page and what came next was this. [Music] Well, this sounds very energetic, doesn't it? So within a couple of minutes, and the piece isn't even finished yet, I experienced two very contrasting characters: beautiful melancholy and sheer energy. And I consider these two elements to be vital human expressions. And the purity of the music makes you hear it very effectively.

Part 2

I've given a lot of children's concerts for children of seven and eight years old, and whatever I play, whether it's Bach, Beethoven, even Stockhausen, or some jazzy music, they are open to hear it, really willing to listen, and they are comfortable doing so. And when classes come in with children who are just a few years older, 11, 12, I felt that I sometimes already had trouble in reaching them like that. The complexity of the music does become an issue, and actually the opinions of others—parents, friends, media—they start to count. But the young ones, they don't question their own opinion. They are in this constant state of wonder, and I do firmly believe that we can keep listening like these seven-year-old children, even when growing up. And that is why I have played not only in the concert hall but also on the street, online, in the air: to feel that state of wonder, to truly listen, and to listen without prejudice. And I would like to invite you to do so now. [music]

Thank you.

Unit 5 Roman Mars: The worst-designed thing you've never noticed

Part 1

I know what you're thinking: "Why does that guy get to sit down?" That's because this is radio.

I tell radio stories about design, and I report on all kinds of stories: buildings and toothbrushes and mascots and wayfinding and fonts. My mission is to get people to engage with the design that they care about so they begin to pay attention to all forms of design.

[…] And few things give me greater joy than a well-designed flag. Yeah! Happy 50th anniversary on your flag, Canada. It is beautiful, gold standard. Love it. I'm kind of obsessed with flags. Sometimes I bring up the topic of flags, and people are like, "I don't care about flags," and then we start talking about flags, and trust me, 100 percent of people care about flags. There's just something about them that works on our emotions.

[…] Okay. So when I moved back to San Francisco in 2008, I researched its flag, because I had never seen it in the previous eight years I lived there. And I found it, I am sorry to say, sadly lacking. I know. It hurts me, too.

Part 2

Narrator: The five basic principles of flag design. Number one.

Flag expert, Ted Kaye: Keep it simple. Narrator: Number two. TK: Use meaningful symbolism.

Narrator: Number three. TK: Use two to three basic colors.

Narrator: Number four. TK: No lettering or seals.

Narrator: Never use writing of any kind. TK: Because you can't read that at a distance.

Narrator: Number five. TK: And be distinctive.

Roman Mars: All the best flags tend to stick to these principles. And like I said before, most country flags are okay. But here's the thing: if you showed this list of principles to any designer of almost anything, they would say these principles—simplicity, deep meaning, having few colors or being thoughtful about colors, uniqueness, don't have writing you can't read—all those principles apply to them, too.

[…] But here's the trick: If you want to design a great flag, a kickass flag like Chicago's or D.C.'s, which also has a great flag, start by drawing a one-by-one-and-a-half-inch rectangle on a piece of paper. Your design has to fit within that tiny rectangle. Here's why.

TK: A three-by-five-foot flag on a pole 100 feet away looks about the same size as a one-by-one-and-a-half-inch rectangle seen about 15 inches from your eye. You'd be surprised at how compelling and simple the design can be when you hold yourself to that limitation.

RM: Meanwhile, back in San Francisco. Is there anything we can do?

TK: I like to say that in every bad flag there's a good flag trying to get out. The way to make San Francisco's flag a good flag is to take the motto off because you can't read that at a distance. Take the name off, and the border might even be made thicker, so it's more a part of the flag. And I would simply take the phoenix and make it a great big element in the middle of the flag.

RM: But the current phoenix, that's got to go.

TK: I would simplify or stylize the phoenix. Depict a big, wide-winged bird coming out of flames. Emphasize those flames.

RM: So this San Francisco flag was designed by Frank Chimero based on Ted Kaye's suggestions. I don't know what he would do if we was completely unfettered and didn't follow those guidelines. Fans of my radio show and podcast, they've heard me complain about bad flags. They've sent me other suggested designs. This one's by Neil Mussett. Both are so much better. And I think if they were adopted, I would see them around the city.

Part 3

TK: Often when city leaders say, "We have more important things to do than worry about a city flag," my response is, "If you had a great city flag, you would have a banner for people to rally under to face those more important things."

[…] So maybe all the city flags can be as inspiring as Hong Kong or Portland or Trondheim, and we can do away with all the bad flags like San Francisco, Milwaukee, Cedar Rapids, and finally, when we're all done, we can do something about Pocatello, Idaho, considered by the North American Vexillological Association as the worst city flag in North America. Yeah. That thing has a trademark symbol on it, people. That hurts me just to look at. Thank you so much for listening.

Unit 6 Jarrett J. Krosoczka: How a boy became an artist

Part 1

When I was in the third grade, a monumental event happened. An author visited our school, Jack Gantos. A published author of books came to talk to us about what he did for a living. And afterwards, we all went back to our classrooms and we drew our own renditions of his main character, Rotten Ralph. And suddenly the author appeared in our doorway, and I remember him sort of sauntering down the aisles, going from kid to kid looking at the desks, not saying a word. But he stopped next to my desk, and he tapped on my desk, and he said, "Nice cat." And he wandered away. Two words that made a colossal difference in my life. When I was in the third grade, I wrote a book for the first time, "The Owl Who Thought He Was The Best Flyer."

[...] So I loved writing so much that I'd come home from school, and I would take out pieces of paper, and I would staple them together, and I would fill those blank pages with words and pictures just because I loved using my imagination. And so these characters would become my friends. There was an egg, a tomato, a head of lettuce and a pumpkin, and they all lived in this refrigerator city, and in one of their adventures they went to a haunted house that was filled with so many dangers like an evil blender who tried to chop them up, an evil toaster who tried to kidnap the bread couple, and an evil microwave who tried to melt their friend who was a stick of butter.

Part 2

So how did I make friends? I drew funny pictures of my teachers — and I passed them around. Well, in English class, in ninth grade, my friend John, who was sitting next to me, laughed a little bit too hard. Mr. Greenwood was not pleased. He instantly saw that I was the cause of the commotion, and for the first time in my life, I was sent to the hall, and I thought, "Oh no, I'm doomed. My grandfather's just going to kill me." And he came out to the hallway and he said, "Let me see the paper." And I thought, "Oh no. He thinks it's a note." And so I took this picture, and I handed it to him. And we sat in silence for that brief moment, and he said to me, "You're really talented." "You're really good. You know, the school newspaper needs a new cartoonist, and you should be the cartoonist. Just stop drawing in my class." So my parents never found out about it. I didn't get in trouble.

[...] I kept making comics, and at the Worcester Art Museum, I was given the greatest piece of advice by any educator I was ever given. Mark Lynch, he's an amazing teacher and he's still a dear friend of mine, and I was 14 or 15, and I walked into his comic book class halfway through the course, and I was so excited, I was beaming. I had this book that was how to draw comics in the Marvel way, and it taught me how to draw superheroes, how to draw a woman, how to draw muscles just the way they were supposed to be if I were to ever draw for X-Men or Spiderman. And all the color just drained from his face, and he looked at me, and he said, "Forget everything you learned." And I didn't understand. He said, "You have a great style. Celebrate your own style. Don't draw the way you're being told to draw. Draw the way you're drawing and keep at it, because you're really good."

Part 3

I graduated from RISD. My grandparents were very proud, and I moved to Boston, and I set up shop. I set up a studio and I tried to get published. I would send out my books. I would send out hundreds of postcards to editors and art directors, but they would go unanswered.

[...] Now, I used to work the weekends at the Hole in the Wall off-season programming to make some extra money as I was trying to get my feet off the ground, and this kid who was just this really hyper kid, I started calling him "Monkey Boy," and I went home and wrote a book called "Good Night, Monkey Boy." And I sent out one last batch of postcards. And I received an email from an editor at Random House with a subject line, "Nice work!" Exclamation point. "Dear Jarrett, I received your postcard. I liked your art, so I went to your website and I'm wondering if you ever tried writing any of your own stories, because I really like your art and it looks like there are some stories that go with them. Please let me know if you're ever in New York City." And this was from an editor at Random House Children's Books. So the next week I "happened" to be in New York. And I met with this editor, and I left New York for a contract for my first book, "Good Night, Monkey Boy," which was published on June 12, 2001.

[...] And then something happened that changed my life. I got my first piece of significant fan mail, where this kid loved Monkey Boy so much that he wanted to have a Monkey Boy birthday cake. For a two-year-old, that is like a tattoo. You know? You only get one birthday per year. And for him, it's only his second. And I got this picture, and I thought, "This picture is going to live within his consciousness for his entire life. He will forever have this photo in his family photo albums." So that photo, since that moment, is framed in front of me while I've worked on all of my books.

[...] And I get the most amazing fan mail, and I get the most amazing projects, and the biggest moment for me came last Halloween. The doorbell rang and it was a trick-or-treater dressed as my character. It was so cool.

Unit 7 Andras Forgacs: Leather and meat without killing animals

Part 1

I'm convinced that in 30 years, when we look back on today and on how we raise and slaughter billions of animals to make our hamburgers and our handbags, we'll see this as being wasteful and indeed crazy. Did you know that today we maintain a global herd of 60 billion animals to provide our meat, dairy, eggs, and leather goods? And over the next few decades, as the world's population expands to 10 billion, this will need to nearly double to 100 billion animals.

But maintaining this herd takes a major toll on our planet. Animals are not just raw materials. They're living beings, and already our livestock is one of the largest users of land, fresh water, and one of the biggest producers of greenhouse gases, which drive climate change. On top of this, when you get so many animals so close together, it creates a breeding ground for disease and opportunities for harm and abuse. Clearly, we cannot continue on this path which puts the environment, public health, and food security at risk. There is another way, . . .

Part 2

There is another way, because essentially, animal products are just collections of tissues, and right now we breed and raise highly complex animals only to create products that are made of relatively simple tissues. What if, instead of starting with a complex and sentient animal, we started with what the tissues are made of, the basic unit of life, the cell? This is biofabrication, where cells themselves can be used to grow biological products like tissues and organs.

[...] And we should begin by reimagining leather. I emphasize leather because it is so widely used. It is beautiful, and it has long been a part of our history. Growing leather is also technically simpler than growing other animal products like meat. It mainly uses one cell type, and it is largely two-dimensional.

Part 3

And so I'm very excited to show you, for the first time, the first batch of our cultured leather, fresh from the lab. This is real, genuine leather, without the animal sacrifice. It can have all the characteristics of leather because it is made of the same cells, and better yet, there is no hair to remove, no scars or insect's bites, and no waste. This leather can be grown in the shape of a wallet, a handbag or a car seat. It is not limited to the irregular shape of a cow or an alligator.

And because we make this material, we grow this leather from the ground up, we can control its properties in very interesting ways. This piece of leather is a mere seven tissue layers thick, and as you can see, it is nearly transparent. And this leather is 21 layers thick and quite opaque. You don't have that kind of fine control with conventional leather.

[…] We can design new materials, new products, and new facilities. We need to move past just killing animals as a resource to something more civilized and evolved. Perhaps we are ready for something literally and figuratively more cultured. Thank you.

Unit 8 Alessandra Orofino: It's our city. Let's fix it.

Part 1

Fifty-four percent of the world's population lives in our cities. In developing countries, one third of that population is living in slums. Seventy-five percent of global energy consumption occurs in our cities, and 80 percent of gas emissions that cause global warming come from our cities. So things that you and I might think about as global problems, like climate change, the energy crisis or poverty, are really, in many ways, city problems. They will not be solved unless people who live in cities, like most of us, actually start doing a better job, because right now, we are not doing a very good one.

[…] Three years ago, I cofounded an organization called Meu Rio, and we make it easier for people in the city of Rio to organize around causes and places that they care about in their own city, and have an impact on those causes and places every day. In these past three years, Meu Rio grew to a network of 160,000 citizens of Rio. About 40 percent of those members are young people aged 20 to 29. That is one in every 15 young people of that age in Rio today.

Part 2

Amongst our members is this adorable little girl, Bia, to your right, and Bia was just 11 years old when she started a campaign using one of our tools to save her model public school from demolition. Her school actually ranks among the best public schools in the country, and it was going to be demolished by the Rio de Janeiro state government to build, I kid you not, a parking lot for the World Cup right before the event happened. Bia started a campaign, and we even watched her school 24/7 through webcam monitoring, and many months afterwards, the government changed their minds. Bia's school stayed in place.

There's also Jovita. She's an amazing woman whose daughter went missing about 10 years ago, and since then, she has been looking for her daughter. In that process, she found out that first, she was not alone. In the last year alone, 2013, 6,000 people disappeared in the state of Rio. But she also found out that in spite of that, Rio had no centralized intelligence system for solving missing persons cases. In other Brazilian cities, those systems have helped solve up to 80 percent of missing persons cases. She started a campaign, and after the secretary of security got 16,000 emails from people asking him to do this, he responded, and started to build a police unit specializing in those cases. It was open to the public at the end of last month, and Jovita was there giving interviews and being very fancy.

And then, there is Leandro. Leandro is an amazing guy in a slum in Rio, and he created a recycling project in the slum. At the end of last year, December 16, he received an eviction order by the Rio de Janeiro state government giving him two weeks to leave the space that he had been using for two years. The plan was to hand it over to a developer, who planned to turn it into a construction site. Leandro started a campaign using one of our tools, the Pressure Cooker, the same one that Bia and Jovita used, and the state government changed their minds before Christmas Eve.

Part 3

These stories make me happy, but not just because they have happy endings. They make me happy because they are happy beginnings. The teacher and parent community at Bia's school is looking for other ways they could improve that space even further. Leandro has ambitious plans to take his model to other low-income communities in Rio, and Jovita is volunteering at the police unit that she helped created.

[…] With the Our Cities network, the Meu Rio team hopes to share what we have learned with other people who want to create similar initiatives in their own cities. We have already started doing it in São Paulo with incredible results, and want to take it to cities around the world through a network of citizen-centric, citizen-led organizations that can inspire us, challenge us, and remind us to demand real participation in our city lives.

It is up to us to decide whether we want schools or parking lots, community-driven recycling projects or construction sites, loneliness or solidarity, cars or buses, and it is our responsibility to do that now, for ourselves, for our families, for the people who make our lives worth living, and for the incredible creativity, beauty, and wonder that make our cities, in spite of all of their problems, the greatest invention of our time. Obrigado. Thank you.

Unit 9 Joy Sun: Should you donate differently?

Part 1

I suspect that every aid worker in Africa comes to a time in her career when she wants to take all the money for her project—maybe it's a school or a training program—pack it in a suitcase, get on a plane flying over the poorest villages in the country, and start throwing that money out the window. Because to a veteran aid worker, the idea of putting cold, hard cash into the hands of the poorest people on Earth doesn't sound crazy, it sounds really satisfying.

[…] Well, why did I spend a decade doing other stuff for the poor? Honestly, I believed that I could do more good with money for the poor than the poor could do for themselves. I held two assumptions: One, that poor people are poor in part because they're uneducated and don't make good choices; two is that we then need people like me to figure out what they need and get it to them. It turns out, the evidence says otherwise.

Part 2

In recent years, researchers have been studying what happens when we give poor people cash. Dozens of studies show across the board that people use cash transfers to improve their own lives. Pregnant women in Uruguay buy better food and give birth to healthier babies. Sri Lankan men invest in their businesses. Researchers who studied our work in Kenya found that people invested in a range of assets, from livestock to equipment to home improvements, and they saw increases in income from business and farming one year after the cash was sent.

Part 3

One very telling study looked at a program in India that gives livestock to the so-called ultra-poor, and they found that 30 percent of recipients had turned around and sold the livestock they had been given for cash. The real irony is, for every 100 dollars' worth of assets this program gave someone, they spent another 99 dollars to do it. What if, instead, we use technology to put cash, whether from aid agencies or from any one of us directly into a poor person's hands.

Part 4

Today, three in four Kenyans use mobile money, which is basically a bank account that can run on any cell phone. A sender can pay a 1.6 percent fee and with the click of a button send money directly to a recipient's account with no intermediaries.

[…] That's what we've started to do at GiveDirectly. We're the first organization dedicated to providing cash transfers to the poor. We've sent cash to 35,000 people across rural Kenya and Uganda in one-time payments of 1,000 dollars per family. So far, we've looked for the poorest people in the poorest villages, and in this part of the world, they're the ones living in homes made of mud and thatch, not cement and iron.

[…] Something that five years ago would have seemed impossible we can now do efficiently and free of corruption. The more cash we give to the poor, and the more evidence we have that it works, the more we have to reconsider everything else we give. Today, the logic behind aid is too often, well, we do at least some good.

[…] What if the logic was, will we do better than cash given directly? Organizations would have to prove that they're doing more good for the poor than the poor can do for themselves. Of course, giving cash won't create public goods like eradicating disease or building strong institutions, but it could set a higher bar for how we help individual families improve their lives.

Unit 10 Tan Le: A headset that reads your brainwaves

Part 1

Up until now, our communication with machines has always been limited to conscious and direct forms. Whether it's something simple like turning on the lights with a switch, or even as complex as programming robotics, we have always had to give a command to a machine, or even a series of commands, in order for it to do something for us. Communication between people, on the other hand, is far more complex and a lot more interesting because we take into account so much more than what is explicitly expressed. We observe facial expressions, body language, and we can intuit feelings and emotions from our dialogue with one another. This actually forms a large part of our decision-making process. Our vision is to introduce this whole new realm of human interaction into human-computer interaction so that computers can understand not only what you direct it to do, but it can also respond to your facial expressions and emotional experiences. And what better way to do this than by interpreting the signals naturally produced by our brain, our center for control and experience.

Part 2

So with that, I'd like to invite onstage Evan Grant, who is one of last year's speakers, who's kindly agreed to help me to demonstrate what we've been able to develop.

[…] So Evan, choose something that you can visualize clearly in your mind.

Evan Grant: Let's do "pull."

Tan Le: Okay, so let's choose "pull." So the idea here now is that Evan needs to imagine the object coming forward into the screen, and there's a progress bar that will scroll across the screen while he's doing that. The first time, nothing will happen, because the system has no idea how he thinks about "pull." But maintain that thought for the entire duration of the eight seconds. So: one, two, three, go. Okay. So once we accept this, the cube is live. So let's see if Evan can actually try and imagine pulling. Ah, good job! That's really amazing.

Part 3

So I'd like to show you a few examples, because there are many possible applications for this new interface. In games and virtual worlds, for example, your facial expressions can naturally and intuitively be used to control an avatar or virtual character. Obviously, you can experience the fantasy of magic and control the world with your mind. And also, colors, lighting, sound, and effects can dynamically respond to your emotional state to heighten the experience that you're having, in real time. And moving on to some applications developed by developers and researchers around the world, with robots and simple machines, for example—in this case, flying a toy helicopter simply by thinking "lift" with your mind.

The technology can also be applied to real world applications—in this example, a smart home. You know, from the user interface of the control system to opening curtains or closing curtains. And of course, also to the lighting—turning them on or off. And finally, to real life-changing applications, such as being able to control an electric wheelchair. In this example, facial expressions are mapped to the movement commands.

[Video] Man: Now blink right to go right. Now blink left to turn back left. Now smile to go straight.

TL: We really—Thank you. We are really only scratching the surface of what is possible today, and with the community's input, and also with the involvement of developers and researchers from around the world, we hope that you can help us to shape where the technology goes from here. Thank you so much.

Unit 11 Louie Schwartzberg: The hidden beauty of pollination

Part 1

It's great being here at TED. You know, I think there might be some presentations that will go over my head, but the most amazing concepts are the ones that go right under my feet. The little things in life, sometimes that we forget about, like pollination, that we take for granted. And you can't tell the story about pollinators—bees, bats, hummingbirds, butterflies—without telling the story about the invention of flowers and how they co-evolved over 50 million years.

I've been filming time-lapse flowers 24 hours a day, seven days a week, for over 35 years. To watch them move is a dance I'm never going to get tired of. It fills me with wonder, and it opens my heart. Beauty and seduction, I believe, is nature's tool for survival, because we will protect what we fall in love with. Their relationship is a love story that feeds the Earth. It reminds us that we are a part of nature, and we're not separate from it.

When I heard about the vanishing bees, Colony Collapse Disorder, it motivated me to take action. We depend on pollinators for over a third of the fruits and vegetables we eat. And many scientists believe it's the most serious issue facing mankind. It's like the canary in the coalmine. If they disappear, so do we. It reminds us that we are a part of nature and we need to take care of it.

Part 2

I realized that nature had invented reproduction as a mechanism for life to move forward, as a life force that passes right through us and makes us a link in the evolution of life. Rarely seen by the naked eye, this intersection between the animal world and the plant world is truly a magic moment. It's the mystical moment where life regenerates itself, over and over again.

So here is some nectar from my film. I hope you'll drink, tweet and plant some seeds to pollinate a friendly garden. And always take time to smell the flowers, and let it fill you with beauty, and rediscover that sense of wonder. Here are some images from the film. [Music]

Thank you. Thank you very much.

Unit 12 Nizar Ibrahim: How we unearthed the *Spinosaurus*

Part 1

These dragons from deep time are incredible creatures. They're bizarre, they're beautiful, and there's very little we know about them. These thoughts were going through my head when I looked at the pages of my first dinosaur book. I was about five years old at the time, and I decided there and then that I would become a paleontologist. Paleontology allowed me to combine my love for animals with my desire to travel to far-flung corners of the world.

And now, a few years later, I've led several expeditions to the ultimate far-flung corner on this planet, the Sahara. I've worked in the Sahara because I've been on a quest to uncover new remains of a bizarre, giant predatory dinosaur called *Spinosaurus*.

A few bones of this animal have been found in the deserts of Egypt and were described about 100 years ago by a German paleontologist. Unfortunately, all his *Spinosaurus* bones were destroyed in World War II. So all we're left with are just a few drawings and notes. From these drawings, we know that this creature, which lived about 100 million years ago, was very big, it had tall spines on its back, forming a magnificent sail, and it had long, slender jaws, a bit like a crocodile, with conical teeth, that may have been used to catch slippery prey, like fish. But that was pretty much all we knew about this animal for the next 100 years.

Part 2

Finally, very recently, we were able to track down a dig site where a local fossil hunter found several bones of *Spinosaurus*. We returned to the site, we collected more bones. And so after 100 years we finally had another partial skeleton of this bizarre creature. And we were able to reconstruct it.

We now know that *Spinosaurus* had a head a little bit like a crocodile, very different from other predatory dinosaurs, very different from the *T. rex*. But the really interesting information came from the rest of the skeleton. We had long spines, the spines forming the big sail. We had leg bones, we had skull bones, we had paddle-shaped feet, wide feet—again, very unusual, no other dinosaur has feet like this—and we think they may have been used to walk on soft sediment, or maybe for paddling in the water. We also looked at the fine microstructure of the bone, the inside structure of *Spinosaurus* bones, and it turns out that they're very dense and compact. Again, this is something we see in animals that spend a lot of time in the water, it's useful for buoyancy control in the water.

We C.T.-scanned all of our bones and built a digital *Spinosaurus* skeleton. And when we looked at the digital skeleton, we realized that yes, this was a dinosaur unlike any other. It's bigger than a *T. rex*, and yes, the head has "fish-eating" written all over it, but

really the entire skeleton has "water-loving" written all over it—dense bone, paddle-like feet, and the hind limbs are reduced in size, and again, this is something we see in animals that spend a substantial amount of time in the water.

Part 3

So, as we fleshed out our *Spinosaurus*—I'm looking at muscle attachments and wrapping our dinosaur in skin—we realize that we're dealing with a river monster, a predatory dinosaur, bigger than *T. rex*, the ruler of this ancient river of giants, feeding on the many aquatic animals I showed you earlier on.

So that's really what makes this an incredible discovery. It's a dinosaur like no other. And some people told me, "Wow, this is a once-in-a-lifetime discovery. There are not many things left to discover in the world." Well, I think nothing could be further from the truth. I think the Sahara's still full of treasures, and when people tell me there are no places left to explore, I like to quote a famous dinosaur hunter, Roy Chapman Andrews, and he said, "Always, there has been an adventure just around the corner—and the world is still full of corners." That was true many decades ago when Roy Chapman Andrews wrote these lines. And it is still true today.

Thank you.

Grammar Summary

UNIT 1: Simple present and present continuous

I'm reading a book about pandas.
She's volunteering at the animal shelter.
They're studying global warming.

I'm not working on my report right now.
She isn't supporting our cause.
They aren't studying owls.

Is the weather changing around here?
Yes, it is. / No, it isn't.
Are panda numbers declining?
Yes, they are. / No, they aren't.

We use the present continuous to talk about …

- events in progress.
  The polar bear is hunting for seals.

- changing situations.
  Polar bear numbers are decreasing.

We use the simple present to talk about …

- habits and routines.
  Seals hunt penguins.

- things that are always true.
  Polar bears have thick fur.

UNIT 2: Future forms

I'm (not) going to be at the reunion.
He's (not) going to come on Friday.
They're (not) going to stay long.

Who are you going to bring?
What time is your sister going to come?
How long are your parents going to stay?

We use both *be going to* and the present continuous to talk about future arrangements.

- *I'm going to see my family this weekend.*
- *I'm seeing my family this weekend.*

We use *be going to* when we want to talk about intentions in the more distant future.

- *I'm going to be a dentist when I'm older.*

UNIT 3: Relative clauses

It's about a young boy. He's a wizard.
It's about a young boy who's a wizard.

He has some friends. They help him.
He has some friends who help him.

I'm reading a book. It's really good.
I'm reading a book that's really good.

That is the place. He grew up there.
That is the place where he grew up.

A relative clause can begin with a pronoun that acts as its subject. The verb agrees with the subject.

- *It's about a wizard who lives at a school.*
- *It's about wizards who live at a school.*

We use *who* to add details to people, *that* to add details to things, and *where* to add details to places.

- *Draco is the one who doesn't like Harry.*
- *Hedwig is an owl that helps Harry.*
- *Hogwarts is the school where he studies.*

UNIT 4: Countable and uncountable nouns

Countable nouns
How many songs can you play on your guitar?
I know a lot of / some / a few songs.
I don't know many / any songs.
There were too many people there.

Uncountable nouns
How much rock music do you have?
I have a lot of / some / a little rock music.
I don't have much / any pop music.
You have too much pop music.

Countable nouns can be singular or plural. Uncountable nouns are always singular.

- *Did you buy one ticket or two tickets?*
- *All their music is very unusual.*

We can use *many* and *a few* before countable nouns and *much* and *a little* before uncountable nouns. We can use *a lot of, some, (not) any*, before either.

- *He doesn't have many / a lot of friends.*
- *He doesn't have much / a lot of money.*

UNIT 5: Prepositions of place

I live in a small house.
The living room is at the top of the stairs.
The door is at the bottom of the stairs.
There is a large blue rug on the floor.
It has a red border around it.
There is a bookshelf on the left / on the right.
A table is to the left of / to the right of the sofa.
There is a TV in front of the sofa.
There is a window behind the sofa.
There is a garage next to my house.
I park my car inside the garage.
There are some trees between my house and my neighbor's house.

We can use prepositions to describe the location of things.

- *There is a picture on the wall.*
- *Your coat is in the closet.*
- *There is a lamp next to the sofa.*

Some prepositions have opposites.

- *The plant is to the left of the table.*
- *The table is to the right of the plant.*

- *The table is in front of the sofa.*
- *The sofa is behind the table.*

UNIT 6: Reported speech

"I need help."
I said (that) I needed help.
I told him (that) I needed help.

"Stop."
I told him to stop.

"Don't continue."
I told him not to continue.

"I want an ice cream."
She said (that) she wanted an ice cream.

"I don't understand."
He said (that) he didn't understand.

When we use *tell*, we name the person that is spoken to. With *say*, we do not.

- *He told me (that) he was sorry.*
- *He said (that) he was sorry.*

We use *tell someone to* when we want to report orders or advice.

- *She told me to be quiet.*
  He told her not to worry.

Present tense verbs often change to a past tense form in reported speech.

- *"I believe in you."*
  He said that he believed in me.

UNIT 7: *Will* for predictions

In 2050, the world population will be around 10 billion.	We use *will* to make predictions about the future.
This will definitely affect the environment. We will probably need to rethink the way we produce food.	• *There will be a greater demand for beef.* We can use *definitely* or *probably* after *will* to make a prediction more or less certain.
It definitely won't be easy. There probably won't be enough space to grow all the crops we need.	• *People will probably / definitely eat less wild fish.* In a negative sentence, *probably* or *definitely* comes before *won't*.
Will the population continue to grow after 2050?	• *I probably / definitely won't change my eating habits.*

UNIT 8: Phrasal verbs

Look out!	Phrasal verbs are usually two-part verbs. The second word gives a new meaning.
Can you look after my plants?	• *Let's take in a movie.* (*take in = see*)
I really look up to him.	
I'll pick the children up from school. I'll pick up the children from school. I'll pick them up. ~~I'll pick up them.~~	With separable verbs, a noun can go between or after the two words. A pronoun must go between them. • *Check this map out. / Check out this map. Check it out. / ~~Check out it.~~*
I don't care for this restaurant. I don't care for it.	With non-separable phrasal verbs, any noun or pronoun must go at the end. • *I'm looking forward to the movie / it.*

UNIT 9: *Will* for offers and conditions

I'll help with the fundraiser. I'll ask my friends to help. Will you ask your brother to help?	We can use *will* (*'ll*) to offer to do something. • *Is that the phone? I'll get it.*
If they come, we'll have enough people. If they don't come, we won't have enough.	We can also use *will* in describing real conditions. The *if* clause is in the present tense and the main clause uses *will*. • *If I give $20, how much will you give?* • *How much will you give if I give $20?*

UNIT 10: Adverbial phrases

Time I try to exercise my brain every day. I find it difficult to study on the weekend. **Manner** He reads slowly. She's studying quietly. **Attitude** Fortunately, the brain scan found no problems. Amazingly, he could do complicated math in just seconds.	Adverbials of time tell us when something happened or will happen. They usually appear at the end of a sentence. • *I went swimming two days ago.* • *I'm going abroad next week.* Adverbs of manner tell us how something happened. They usually appear after the main verb or the object. • *They worked quietly.* • *She completed the puzzle quickly.* Adverbs of attitude express the speaker's attitude toward an action. They are usually at the beginning of a sentence. • *Interestingly, your brain can't feel pain.*

UNIT 11: Present perfect

I've been to Europe. She's traveled overseas three times. They've visited a farm before. I haven't been hiking before. She hasn't climbed many trees They've never seen a wild animal. Have you ever ridden a horse? Yes, I have. / No, I haven't. Has your friend ever swum in the ocean? Yes, she has. / No, she hasn't.	We use the present perfect to talk about experiences. • *I've climbed Mount Fuji.* • *I've never been to Okinawa.* • *Have you ever climbed a mountain?* When we provide details about an experience, we usually use the simple past. • *I climbed it two years ago.* • *I went there with my best friend.*

UNIT 12: Passive

King Tut is known by many people as the Boy King. Roman coins are found throughout Europe. The site was discovered in 1949. The bones were put on display. Is the statue covered in gold? Yes, it is. / No, it isn't. Are the weapons made of iron? Yes, they are. / No, they aren't.	We use the passive voice … • to change the focus of a sentence. *Hans Sloane founded the British Museum.* *The British Museum was founded by Hans Sloane* • when we don't know who performs an action. *The castle was burned to the ground.* • when it's obvious or not important who performs the action. *The dinosaur bones were found in Africa.*

Acknowledgements

The Author and Publisher would like to thank the following teaching professionals for their valuable input during the development of this series:

Coleeta Paradise Abdullah, Certified Training Center; **Tara Amelia Arntsen**, Northern State University; **Estela Campos**; **Federica Castro**, Pontificia Universidad Católica Madre y Maestra; **Amy Cook**, Bowling Green State University; **Carrie Cheng**, School of Continuing and Professional Studies, the University of Hong Kong; **Mei-ho Chiu**, Soochow University; **Anthony Sean D'Amico**, SDH Institute; **Wilder Yesid Escobar Almeciga**, Universidad El Bosque; **Rosa E. Vasquez Fernandez**, English for International Communication; **Touria Ghaffari**, The Beekman School; **Rosario Giraldez**, Alianza Cultural Uruguay Estados Unidos; **William Haselton**, NC State University; **Yu Huichun**, Macau University of Science and Technology; **Michelle Kim**, TOPIA Education; **Jay Klaphake**, Kyoto University of Foreign Studies; **Kazuteru Kuramoto**, Keio Senior High School; **Michael McCollister**, Feng Chia University; **Jennifer Meldrum**, EC English Language Centers; **Holly Milkowart**, Johnson County Community College; **Nicholas Millward**, Australian Centre for Education; **Stella Maris Palavecino**, Buenos Aires English House; **Youngsun Park**, YBM; **Adam Parmentier**, Mingdao High School; **Jennie Popp**, Universidad Andrés Bello; **Terri Rapoport**, ELS Educational Services; **Erich Rose**, Auburn University; **Yoko Sakurai**, Aichi University; **Mark D. Sheehan**, Hannan University; **DongJin Shin**, Hankuk University of Foreign Studies; **Shizuka Tabara**, Kobe University; **Jeffrey Taschner**, AUA Language Center; **Hadrien Tournier**, Berlitz Corporation; **Rosa Vasquez**, JFK Institute; **Jindarat De Vleeschauwer**, Chiang Mai University; **Tamami Wada**, Chubu University; **Colin Walker**, Myongii University; **Elizabeth Yoon**, Hanyang University; **Keiko Yoshida**, Konan University

And special thanks to: **Tony Gainsford, Neil Glover, Fredrik Hiebert, Mary Kadera, Sarah Lafferty, Ken Lejtenyi, Joel Sartore, Barton Seaver, Claire Street, Madeleine Thien**

Credits

Photo Credits

Cover © Patrick Bingham Hall, **3** Thomas J. Abercrombie/National Geographic Creative, **4** (tl) © Munir Virani, (tr) © Marla Aufmuth/TED, (cl) © James Duncan Davidson/TED, (cr) © Handel At The Piano, (bl) © Bret Hartman/TED, (br) Boston Globe/Getty Images, **5** (tl) (tr) © James Duncan Davidson/TED, (cl) © Ryan Lash/TED, (cr) (bl) © James Duncan Davidson/TED, (br) © TED, **6** (tl1) Joel Sartore, National Geographic Photo ARK/National Geographic Creative, (tl2) Joel Sartore/National Geographic Creative, (cl1) Thomas J. Abercrombie / National Geographic Creative, (cl2) PeopleImages.com/DigitalVision/Getty Images, (bl1) The Washington Post/Getty Images, (bl2) Greg Dale/National Geographic Creative, **8** (tl1) Design Pics Inc/National Geographic Creative, (tl2) Richard Nowitz/National Geographic Creative, (cl1) Kike Calvo/National Geographic Creative, (cl2) Sebastian Kaulitzki/Shutterstock.com, (bl1) Design Pics Inc/National Geographic Creative, (bl2) Denis Gliksman/Inrap/Abacapress.com/Newscom, **10–11** © James Duncan Davidson/TED, **12** © Michael Brands/TED, **13** © Munir Virani, **14** Joel Sartore, National Geographic Photo ARK/National Geographic Creative, **15** Joel Sartore/National Geographic Creative, **17** Gallo Images/Getty Images, **18** Joel Sartore/National Geographic Creative, **20** © TED, **21** Joel Sartore/National Geographic Creative, **22** (tl) Joel Sartore, National Geographic Photo ARK/National Geographic Creative, (tr) Danita Delimont Creative/Alamy Stock Photo, (cl) Brian J. Skerry/National Geographic Creative, (cr) Joel Sartore/National Geographic Creative, **23** © Marla Aufmuth/TED, **24** Blend Images/Alamy Stock Photo, **25** © Ken Lejtenyi, **27** Stacy Gold/National Geographic Creative, **28** Diana Haronis dianasphotoart.com/Moment Select/Getty Images, **30** © Marla Aufmuth/TED, **31** © Elana Goodridge, **32** Blend Images/Alamy Stock Photo, **33** © James Duncan Davidson/TED, **34** Thomas J. Abercrombie/National Geographic Creative, **35** Ullstein Bild/Getty Images, **37** © Harper Collins Publishers. All rights reserved, **38** (tr) © Geopoetika, (cl) © Penguin Books India, (br) © Milkweed Editions, a nonprofit, literary publisher. All rights reserved, **40–41** © James Duncan Davidson/TED, **42** © Hogarth, an imprint of the Crown Publishing Group, a division of Penguin Random House LLC, New York. All rights reserved, **43** © Cengage Learning, **45** © Handel at The Piano, **46** PeopleImages.com/DigitalVision/Getty Images, **47** Hiroyuki Ito/Hulton Archive/Getty Images, **49** Lucy Nicholson/Reuters, **50** Hill Street Studios/Blend Images/Getty Images, **52–53** © James Duncan Davidson/TED, **54** Caroline von Tuempling/The Image Bank/Getty Images, **55** © Bret Hartman/TED, **56** Nikki Kahn/The Washington Post/Getty Images, **57** © Sarah Lafferty, **59** (tl) Squareplum/Shutterstock.com, (tc) Geff Reis/AGE fotostock, (tr) Manon van Os/Shutterstock.com, (cr) ollo/E+/Getty Images, **60** Daniel Stein/iStock/Getty Images Plus/Getty Images, **62** (tr) © Bret Hartman/TED, (cl) Sagid/Shutterstock.com, (cr) Wasan Ritthawon/Shutterstock.com, **64** (tl) Wasan Ritthawon/Shutterstock.com, (tc) Wasan Ritthawon/Shutterstock.com, (tr) Juergen Priewe/Dreamstime.com, **65** Essdras M Suarez/The Boston Globe/Getty Images, **66** Greg Dale/National Geographic Creative, **67** John B. Carnett/Bonnier Corporation/Getty Images, **69** Bettmann/Getty Images, **70** (t) John Leyba/The Denver Post/Getty Images, (cr) © Dragonfly Books, **72–73** © TED, **75** © Cengage Learning, **77** © James Duncan Davidson/TED, **78** Design Pics, Inc./National Geographic Creative, **79** Marvin Joseph/The Washington Post/Getty Images, **81** David McNew/Getty Images News/Getty Images, **82** Curioso/Shutterstock.com, **83** © TED, **84–85** © James Duncan Davidson/TED, **86** Sara Winter/Shutterstock.com, **87** © James Duncan Davidson/TED, **88** Richard Nowitz/National Geographic Creative, **89** © Cengage Learning, **91** Design Pics, Inc./National Geographic Creative, **92** Mike Theiss/National Geographic Creative, **94** © James Duncan Davidson/TED, **95** Donatas Dabravolskas/Shutterstock.com, **96** Philippe Hays/Alamy Stock Photo, **97** © Ryan Lash/TED, **98** Kike Calvo/National Geographic Creative, **99** Neil Glover, **101** D8nn/Shutterstock.com, **102** AP Images/Ariana Cubillos, **104** © Ryan Lash/TED, **105** © TED, **106** Design Pics, Inc./National Geographic Creative, **107** © Cengage Learning, **109** © James Duncan Davidson/TED, **110** Sebastian Kaulitzki/Shutterstock.com, **111** National Geographic Channel/National Geographic Partners, **113** Lionel Bonavenure/AFP/Getty Images, **114** Fabrizio Bensch/Reuters, **116–117** © James Duncan Davidson/TED, **118** Emotiv Lifesciences/National Geographic Creative, **119** © James Duncan Davidson/TED, **120** Design Pics, Inc./National Geographic Creative, **121** © Anthony Gainsford, **123** Kyle Johnson/The New York Times/Redux, **124** Al Petteway & Amy White/National Geographic Creative, **126** © James Duncan Davidson/TED, **127** Frans Lanting/National Geographic Creative, **128** Bill Hatcher/National Geographic Creative, **129** © TED, **130** Abaca/Newscom, **131** Rebecca Hale/National Geographic Creative, **133** Universal History Archive/UIG/Getty Images, **134** Kat Keene Hogue/National Geographic Creative, **136** © TED, **137** Davide Bonadonna/National Geographic Creative, **138** Kenneth Garrett/National Geographic Creative, **139** © Cengage Learning, **141** (tl) Steve Winter/National Geographic Creative, (cl) (bc) Joel Sartore, National Geographic Photo Ark/National Geographic Creative, **142** (tl) Joel Sartore, National Geographic Photo Ark/National Geographic Creative, (cl) Steve Winter/National Geographic Creative, (bc) Danita Delimont Creative/Alamy Stock Photo, **144** Brian J. Skerry/National Geographic Creative, **145** Ira Block/National Geographic Creative, **146** (tl) Alberto Tirado/Shutterstock.com, (cl) Joel Sartore/National Geographic Creative, **147** (t) Giuseppe Cacace/AFP/Getty Images, (c) Fred Dufour/AFP/Getty Images

Illustration & Infographic Credits

16, 26, 36, 48, 58, 68, 80, 90, 100, 112, 122, 132 emc design; **125** Geoffrey Smith

Data sources for infographics: **16** www.worldwildlife.org, **26** www.guinnessworldrecords.com, **36** www.goodreads.com, **58** www.familynamesonline.com, **68** www.raconteur.net, **80** www.nationalgeographic.com, **90** www.rd.com, **100** www.npengage.com, **112** www.nursingassistantcentral.com, www.bebrainfit.com, **122** www.dailywhat.org.uk, **132** news.nationalgeographic.com

Text Credits

18 Source of data: "Vultures are revolting. Here's why we need to save them": ngm.nationalgeographic.com, January 2016, "Why Africa's vultures are collapsing toward extinction": news.nationalgeographic.com, July 2016, **50** Adapted from "Why does music feel so good?": phenomena.nationalgeographic.com, April 2013, **124** Source of data: "Love is in the air": ngm.nationalgeographic.com, December 2009, **134** Adapted from "Nizar Ibrahim, Paleontologist": www.nationalgeographic.com